Tallahassee Gardening:

Design & Care of the Southern Landscape

Published by
Tallahassee Democrat, Inc.
P.O. Box 990
Tallahassee, FL 32302

Book design and layout:
Ken Allewelt, Lori Leath Smith

First printing 1991
Second printing 1994

Library of Congress Catalog Card Number: 94-060598
ISBN: 0-9613040-5-7

Printed in the United States of America

~

This book is dedicated to my parents. To my mother, my best gardening friend, whose flower gardens I have enjoyed since my earliest years. And, to my father who shared with me his love of the outdoors and the land. He passed away in December while working outdoors on our family farm.

~

Acknowledgments

Many people had an influence on the content of this book in one way or another. I'm hesitant to list names, because I can't list everyone. But I would like to list a few special ones anyway.

Allan Armitage
Victoria Christian
Keith Collinsworth
Tim Crocker
Alex and Vicki Cureton
Gene Ellis
Ralph Esposito
Ed Gilman
Bud Heist
George Henry
Gary Knox
Donna Legare
Sydney Park-Brown
Dan Prosser
Stan Rosenthal
Ken Swanson
Jody Walthall
Sue Watkins
Paul Wills

I would also like to thank the Cooperative Extension Service of the University of Florida and Leon County for a career that has given me wonderful experience over the past eighteen years. The Extension Service, which is a cooperative effort between the U.S.D.A., the land grant universities, and county governments, is a tremendous educational service to the citizens of this country.

I'm also grateful to the Master Gardeners of the Leon County Extension Office for their help through the years in maintaining our flower trials. From the trials, we've learned much about what will and will not grow well in our climatic zone.

And, at the *Tallahassee Democrat*, I would like to thank Ray Green, Ken Allewelt, Steve Cannon, Kelly Broderick and Christie Rewiski.

Ray Green was the driving force behind this project, giving me the opportunity to revise and reprint this book. Ken Allewelt designed the cover and inside color pages and was the real workhorse behind the project. Steve Cannon shot the cover photo and several inside color photos and Kelly Broderick's proofreading in a pinch helped a messy manuscript turn into a book ready for printing. Finally, Christie Rewiski was the person responsible for pulling all the loose ends together and keeping the project on schedule.

The *Democrat* team made this edition of the book a big improvement over the original edition. Thank you.

Thanks also to Vicki and Alex Cureton for the use of their beautiful garden as the setting for the cover shot.

Contents

1

Month-By-Month

Maintaining Your Landscape

Knowing when to do things is just about as important in landscape maintenance as knowing what to do. Alhough it doesn't include every little detail, the following timetable is intended to give you an idea of the timing for various landscape maintenance activities throughout the year. Details of these activities follow in the remainder of this book.

Keep in mind that you can be flexible with most of the pointers on the timetable. For example, if you don't fertilize your lawn in April, you can still do it in May. But, try to stick to the schedule as much as possible.

JANUARY-FEBRUARY

Weather: January and February are the heart of our winter in zone 8. Low temperatures can vary from very rare hard freezes in the single digits to mild weather where the low is in the 50's. Similarly, high temperatures can range from a few rare days where the temperature may stay near or below freezing to days with highs in the 80's. Highs in the 50's or 60's are more common though, as are lows in the 30's or 40's.

Rainfall amounts will vary across the zone. However, January and February are not typically dry months. Rainfall is usually sufficient enough that little supplemental irrigation will be required.

In flower during this period may be Taiwan cherries, Japanese magnolias, red maples, redbuds, red buckeyes, camellias, spireas, pansies, sweet alyssum, and spring-flowering bulbs such as daffodils or tulips. If the weather is mild, petunias and snapdragons may be flowering also.

Planting/Transplanting: Plant or transplant woody plants such as shrubs or trees. Now, while it's cool and plants are somewhat dormant, is one of the best times of the year for planting and transplanting. Remember, though, that plants still need water during the winter. Irrigate if rainfall doesn't supply adequate water.

Plant bare-root fruit trees and bare-root roses.

Tulips and many other spring-flowering bulbs can be planted in January. Tulips and hyacinths should have been pre-chilled in your refrigerator for 6-8 weeks immediately before planting.

Many cool-season vegetables can be planted.

February is a good time to divide crowded clumps of perennials.

Pruning: Prune fruit trees and grape vines before late February.

Prune crape myrtles now so they'll be ready in spring for setting buds for summer bloom.

Most evergreen plants can be pruned in late February. For spring-flowering plants, such as azaleas, wait until after they finish flowering.

Prune roses in mid-February.

Fertilization: Fertilize most fruit trees in early to mid-February.

Pest Management: In January, dormant oil sprays may be applied to fruit trees that had a problem with scale insects the previous year.

In February, as fruit tree flower buds begin swelling, start preventative pest control sprays with home orchard sprays available from your garden center.

Lawn Care: If you wish to apply a pre-emergent herbicide to your lawn, do so in late February or early March. Follow label directions carefully.

MARCH-APRIL

Weather: Depending on your exact location, the last killing frost should be in mid to late March. That's not to say, though, that freezing weather can't come as late as April. It's just that it's not very likely in the Deep South.

By late April, daytime temperatures have usually become quite warm, well into the 80's, in much of our zone.

Rainfall is usually adequate for established plants at this time of year because temperatures haven't become extreme.

In flower in early March may be plums, crabapples, pears, peaches, Carolina jessamine, and some spring-flowering bulbs such as daffodils. By mid-March, the dogwoods, silverbells, hawthorns, and azaleas have often started flowering. By mid-April, the fringe trees are usually blooming. March and April also usually bring the first flowers on a number of perennial and annual flowers.

Planting/Transplanting: In late March you can begin planting warm-season vegetables and flowers. In April is a better time for planting caladiums and vinca.

You can continue planting shrubs, trees, flowers, etc., in the warm spring weather. The sooner in spring you plant, though, the better, so that the plants will face less heat stress.

Pruning: Before mid-March you should complete any needed pruning of landscape plants with the exception of spring-flowering plants such as azaleas. Wait until they've finished flowering to prune them.

March is the ideal time to do any renovation pruning of overgrown shrubs.

Fertilization: Fertilize trees and shrubs as needed in early March or late February. Roses will need monthly fertilization throughout the spring and summer.

Fertilize flowers, both perennial and newly planted annuals. Fertilize most annuals monthly through the spring and summer.

Sidedress most vegetables with fertilizer a month or so after they are up and growing.

Lawn Care: Don't fertilize your lawn until after mid-March. And, don't fertilize it then unless it's been at least three weeks since it greened up. There's no rush. The lawn will fare just fine if you wait until April to fertilize it.

Lawngrass can be planted from sod, plugs, sprigs, or seed. The seed, though, will be easier to start after the soil warms considerably in late April, or even later.

Aerate compacted lawns with a mechanical core-type lawn aerator.

If weeds are a serious enough problem in your lawn that you need to apply a post-emergent herbicide, do so before the temperatures start soaring in late April or May. Herbicides shouldn't be applied after temperatures start hovering in the upper 80's.

As you begin mowing the lawn, sharpen the mower blades every 4-6 weeks.

Live oak leaves are falling now. Use them for mulch in flower beds and around trees and shrubs.

MAY

Weather: Basically, May's activities are about the same as April's. Freeze danger is past. But, the rising temperatures, into the 80's and 90's, begin to make starting plants a little more difficult. New plantings will require careful attention to watering. Though there may be enough rain in May, often there are some dry periods and you may even need to begin watering established plantings and the lawn.

In flower: As the cool-season plants that were blooming in March or April finish their flowering now, their color will be replaced by the flowers of warm-season annuals, such as impatiens or begonias, or perennials such as blue salvia or purple coneflowers. Petunias and snapdragons should be flowering well now, too.

A few shrubs such as oakleaf hydrangea, Satsuki azaleas, abelia, oleander and ligustrum may be flowering, too. Southern magnolias, Ashe magnolias, and Jerusalem thorns are trees that may have started flowering.

Planting: You can still plant most shrubs, flowers, and trees from containers. But, pay special attention to watering because of the warm weather.

It's too late to plant many vegetables, though some heat-loving vegetables such as eggplant, okra, southern peas, peppers, and sweet potatoes can still be planted.

Fertilization: Don't forget to fertilize annual flowers and roses monthly throughout the growing season.

Apply side-dressings of fertilizer to most vegetables.

Lawn Care: As the soil temperatures have risen, now is a good time for planting seed for grasses such as centipede. Sod can be easily started, too. Pay careful attention to watering. It's probably too hot now for herbicide application on lawns.

JUNE-JULY

Weather: This is the heart of our summer. Temperatures may be well into the 90's and humidity will be high. July is usually our wettest month. You'll probably find it necessary to water only shallowly rooted annual flowers occasionally when temperatures are high and there is no rain for a week or so. The soil surface can dry quickly in the extreme heat. But, plants with deeper roots such as lawns or established shrub plantings will probably need little irrigation this time of year.

In flower: All of the typical summer-flowering annuals and perennials should be in bloom now. (See the chapter on flowers for more details.) Crape myrtles, magnolias, mimosas, Jerusalem thorns, goldenrain trees, and sourwoods are among trees that may be in flower now. Abelia, althea, gardenia, and oleander are among flowering shrubs of the season.

Planting/Transplanting: Because of the heat, it's not our peak planting season. You can still plant container-grown trees and shrubs, but water faithfully. You can still plant some flowers successfully, but you should plant only those that can really take the heat.

Pruning: Be pinching back chrysanthemums and other fall-blooming perennials now so that bushier plants and more flowers will result. Stop the pinching in August.

Groom perennial flowers that have finished flowering. Remove old flowers, cutting back to

vigorous growth.

Crape myrtles will be in full bloom during this period. After the flowers fade, if you'll cut off the tips of the branches just below the faded flowers, the crape myrtle will produce more flowers.

Formal hedges and other tightly clipped plants can be pruned as needed.

Fertilization: Continue fertilizing annual flowers and roses monthly.

Many fruit trees should be fertilized again now. (See fruit tree chapter for details.)

Pest Management: Now is especially the time to watch for insect and disease pests. Populations increase rapidly this time of year. Aphids on crape myrtles are a common insect pest.

Lawn Care: Watch for spittlebug problems in centipede lawns and chinch bug problems in St. Augustine grass lawns, especially as we move into July.

AUGUST

Weather: By August, our landscape is usually beginning to show signs of wear from summer's heat and humidity. The weather is very similar to that of July, hot and humid, usually with plenty of rain.

In flower: Abelias, crape myrtles, oleanders, altheas, chaste trees, and Jerusalem thorns may be in flower now. Also, many annual and perennial flowers will be blooming, too, though heat and humidity will likely be making them look tired and ragged.

Planting/Transplanting: You can begin planting your fall vegetable garden in late August.

As in June or July, August is not the most ideal planting weather. Still, if careful attention is given to watering should rainfall not be adequate, most container-grown trees and shrubs can be planted.

Heat-tolerant flowers such as melampodium or *Zinnia angustifolia* can be planted.

Pruning: Because summer can be hard on many flowering plants, we need to spend a little extra time grooming plants now. If you take the time to cut back annuals, such as impatiens, that have become leggy over the summer, they'll soon be much more attractive and their flowering life will be extended.

Many perennial flowers, such as 'Indigo Spires' salvia, will also benefit from being trimmed back now, too.

Trim the old faded flower stems off hydrangeas.

Give shrubs with lanky, untidy growth their last pruning of the season.

Fertilization: Now is a good time to fertilize shrubs and small trees again if you're trying to encourage growth.

Don't forget to fertilize annual flowers and roses.

Lawn Care: If your lawn looks fine, don't fertilize it again now. But, if it looks a little weak, now is a good time to fertilize again. The nutrients from the spring fertilization have long since been used or washed away.

Watch for spittlebug problems in centipede grass lawns.

September

Weather: Temperatures begin to drop slightly in September, especially during the night. In the air, there's a slight hint of fall and cooler weather to come. Rainfall amounts also decrease quite a bit. You may have to water established plantings should we go for an extended period without rain.

In flower: September finds many of the same warm-season flowers blooming, but a few new perennials such as pineapple sage, sweet autumn clematis, Mexican sage, 'Autumn Joy' sedum, goldenrod, chrysanthemums, and autumn sage join the list for the next couple of months.

Planting: Plant chrysanthemums for fall bloom.

Plant annuals such as petunias, snapdragons, or even marigolds, for the cooler weather.

September is a good time to divide crowded clumps of perennials.

Continue planting your fall vegetable garden.

Most trees and shrubs can be planted now.

Fertilization: Continue monthly fertilization of annual flowers and roses.

Lawn Care: You may still fertilize your lawn this month but not later.

Watch for sod webworm problems in lawns.

Continue watering your plants and lawn as needed. Don't neglect them now, thinking they should be going dormant and needing no water. It's still early.

October

Weather: October is our driest month. Though days can still be quite warm, in the upper 80's or into the 90's, there is a trend toward cooling. By the end of the month, nights can be quite cool, though we usually don't reach freezing temperatures in October.

In flower: October finds many of the same plants flowering as in September. The fragrant tea olive and the yellow-flowering shrub or small tree, cassia, join the list. Swamp sunflower, with its bright yellow flowers, also demands attention.

Planting/Transplanting: Continue planting your fall vegetable garden. Now is the time to plant strawberries. Now, as temperatures begin moderating again, is a good time for planting trees and shrubs. Just remember to water.

Now is also a good time for transplanting or dividing perennial flowers.

Plant fall annual flowers such as pansies, snapdragons, dianthus, and calendulas.

Fertilization: Continue monthly fertilization of annual flowers and roses.

Don't forget sidedressing fertilizer in the vegetable garden.

Lawn Care: If winter weeds are always a serious problem in your lawn, and you need to apply a pre-emergent herbicide, now is the time.

Continue watering as needed. October is often very dry and water will likely be needed on lawns and other plantings.

November

Weather: The weather finally really starts to feel like fall in November. There will be some very cool nights. There may even be some frost, particularly after mid-month. Days may be cooler, too, but temperatures can still climb into the upper 80's during mild weather. Rainfall may be in short supply, but you still probably won't find it necessary to irrigate established plantings much, because the temperatures will also be lower. However, pay special attention to the water requirements of new plantings.

In flower: Many of the warm-season annuals and perennials will still be in flower until a heavy frost stops them. The perennials, such as pineapple sage, autumn sage, etc., that started flowering in September will also still be in flower. Also joining the flowering list this month should be cool-season annuals such as pansies, snapdragons, dianthus, and petunias. Some camellias may also be in bloom this month. Tea olives, with their pleasing fragrance, should be flowering, too.

Planting/Transplanting: Lots to do in the garden this month! It's a great planting month: shrubs, trees, perennial flowers, cool-season annual flowers, etc.

Plant seeds of such spring-blooming flowers as poppies, bachelor buttons, sweet peas, and sweet alyssum.

Buy spring-flowering bulbs and begin chilling them for 6-8 weeks in your refrigerator before planting.

Continue planting cool-season vegetables in the vegetable garden.

Collect pine straw and leaves for mulching trees, shrubs, flower beds, and vegetable gardens.

Lawn Care: Plant rye grass for temporary green lawn during the winter if desired. Remember, though, you'll have to mow it.

DECEMBER

Weather: December's temperatures are not usually too harsh. There will be nights when the temperature drops below freezing, but there will also be unseasonably warm, humid nights when the temperature stays in the 50's. Sometimes, though, especially late in the month, around Christmas, the cold Arctic air reaches into our area, sending temperatures plummeting into the 20's or even lower. Be prepared for anything during our winter. "Variable, but usually mild," is the best way to describe the weather of our winters. Rainfall usually starts to increase a little in December over the drier October and November.

Plants don't use as much water during the winter, but they still need some. If we don't have much rain, remember that plants will still need watering.

In flower: Camellias should be very colorful by now. The cool-season annuals such as pansies should be very attractive now. Petunias, snapdragons, and dianthus also should stay very colorful throughout the winter unless killed by extreme freezes. Plants with colorful berries, such as hollies, nandinas, and ardesias will add to the season's color. The tea olive will flower on through the winter as long as it's not too cold.

Planting/Transplanting: December is also a good planting month. Almost everything that could be planted in November can be planted now unless we're having a very cold winter. Even if it's very cold, most trees and shrubs can be planted. In fact, now is a

better time for planting trees and shrubs than is June, July, or August. The heat is more stressful on new plants than is the cold.

Continue collecting mulch materials and renewing mulch in beds.

You can begin planting spring-flowering bulbs such as daffodils. Be sure that those such as tulips and hyacinths have been pre-chilled in your refrigerator first.

Pruning: Now is a good time to prune hollies and junipers so that you can use the cuttings for holiday decorations.

Lawn Care: Rye grass lawns can still be planted this month.

Holiday plants: Remember when taking your Christmas tree home to re-cut the base of the stump and place the tree in a bucket of water for 24 hours before placing it inside the house. This is so it will begin absorbing water before you place it in its stand indoors. Keep it watered regularly.

Pick out a poinsettia for the holidays, but keep it out of drafts inside your home so it will hold its bracts longer.

PLAN FOR COLOR THROUGHOUT THE YEAR

Each new season in Tallahassee is heralded by flowers. With careful planning, you can have something blooming in your garden throughout most of the year. You must plan ahead, though. Perhaps the following ideas will be helpful. And, if you're observant throughout the year, I'm sure you can add many others to this list.

❀ **Late winter (typically January-February to early March)**

Camellia - The beautiful evergreen shrubs that have a variety of pink, red, or white flowers fall through spring. Visit Maclay Gardens to see them at their peak in February.

Flowering apricot - Small deciduous tree with pink flowers. About the earliest to flower, often in January.

Taiwan cherry - Earliest flowering cherry, very dark pink. Late January or early February.

Japanese magnolia - Several different species of this deciduous magnolia. Pink, lavender, wine, or white flowers. Usually start in February.

Redbud - Deciduous native tree with brilliant

purplish-pink blooms.

Red maple - Deciduous native tree with red to rust flowers and seeds. Some have better color than others.

Jasminum messnyi - Cascading shrub with yellow flowers you see from late January until March.

Carolina jessamine - Native vine that lights up the woods with its yellow flowers and wonderful fragrance.

Annuals, bulbs, and perennials - Pansies, petunias, dianthus, sweet alyssum, calendulas, narcissus, daffodils, snowdrops, scilla, tulips, and creeping phlox.

❀ Early Spring (typically March - April)

Pears - White flowers. The fruiting pears sometimes bloom in February. The ornamental Bradford pears don't flower well here except after cold winters.

Plums - Chickasaw (shrubby tree) and American plum (larger) both have white flowers.

Crabapple - Small native tree with delicate pink flowers.

Silverbell - Underused small native tree with white flowers.

Dogwoods - Sorry, only the white ones do consistently well here.

Flowering quince - Deciduous shrub with red flowers.

Viburnum tinus - Showy white flowers on a mid-sized attractive evergreen shrub. Flowers may begin in February.

Forsythia - Deciduous shrub with yellow flowers (if enough winter chilling received).

Spirea - Several species of this popular wispy, deciduous shrub exist. Beautiful white flowers.

Azaleas - Several species are used here. Most popular are the large Indica types with flowers of violet, red, white, or pink. Others are mid-sized or smaller. Several native deciduous species exist, with orange, pink, or white flowers. Some very fragrant.

Banana shrub - Yellow flowers that resemble small bananas and that have a very sweet fragrance.

Wisteria - Chinese, the common type, and Japanese, showier and more fragrant, are available. Both vines typically have purple-blue flowers.

Lady Banksia rose - Numerous yellow flowers on this climbing rose.

Annuals and perennials - Poppies, bachelor buttons, larkspur, and sweet peas will be flowering only if you planted from seed in October or November. Woodland phlox, geraniums, snapdragons, dianthus, sweet alyssums, petunias, annual phlox, Louisiana iris.

❀ Late spring (typically April-May, into June)

Fringetree or granddaddy greybeard - Small native tree with clouds of white flowers.

Satsuki azaleas - Small, late-blooming azaleas.

Southern magnolia - Begins flowering in late May to early June.

Oakleaf hydrangea - Native hydrangea with large clusters of white flowers.

Garden hydrangeas - Common hydrangeas with large blue or pink flowers.

Gardenia - Fragrant white flowers on glossy evergreen shrub.

Confederate jasmine - Small, fragrant flowers on an evergreen vine.

Butterfly bush - Large perennial, attractive to butterflies with its blue, purple, lavender, or white spikes.

Annuals - Begonias, impatiens, marigolds, salvia, petunias, geraniums, cosmos, ageratum, cleome, snapdragon, nicotiana, lobelia, and zinnias.

Perennials - Daylilies, amaryllis, cannas, gerbera daisy, lantana, verbena, 'Indigo Spires' salvia, stokesia, phlox, Shasta daisy, coreopsis, and veronica.

❀ Summer

Crape myrtle - Brilliant clusters of red, pink, white, purple, or lavender flowers on these small deciduous trees.

Vitex or Chastetree - Small, deciduous tree with purplish-blue, fragrant flowers. Should be used more.

Jerusalem thorn - Small tree, sometimes damaged by cold in severe winters. Brilliant yellow flowers, but also thorns.

Goldenrain tree - small tree with showy yellow flowers.

Sourwood - Small native tree with white flowers.

Oleander - Tough, durable shrub for hot, sunny sites. Pink, red, yellow, or white flowers. Don't eat any part of the plant. It's very poisonous.

Abelia - Several types of this durable shrub are available. Flowers are either white or pink. Leaves are very glossy and take on almost a burgundy color in full sun.

Clethra - Rapidly becoming more popular, this native shrub and its various cultivars have very fragrant white flowers.

Althea or Rose-of-Sharon - Pink, blue, or white flowers on this large deciduous member of the Hibiscus genus.

Honeysuckles - Several, such as coral honeysuckle, flower from spring through summer with dark pink or gold flowers.

Tough annuals for the summer heat - *Zinnia angustifolia*, gomphrena, melampodium, vinca, portulaca, four o'clocks, thunbergia (vining), and pentas.

Perennials - Verbena, butterfly bush, purple coneflower, jacobinia (shade), shrimp plant, lantana, plumbago, rudbeckia, agapanthus, Mexican heather, and 'Indigo Spires' salvia.

❀ Fall

Cassia - Several species of this small tree with brilliant yellow flowers are available. Some will not overwinter here but are worth planting for the one-year show.

Tea olive - This evergreen shrub has very fragrant, small white flowers not only in the fall, but also in the spring and late winter.

Sasanqua camellias - These are typically the smaller-flowered and earlier blooming camellias.

Sweet autumn clematis - Vine with clouds of fragrant white flowers.

American beautyberry - Flowers aren't showy, but the bright purple berries in the fall are. Small native deciduous shrub.

Annuals - Marigolds, petunias, pansies, dianthus, pentas, and snapdragons.

Perennials - Pineapple sage, firespike (*Odontonema*), plumbago, autumn sage, Mexican sage, chrysanthemums, swamp sunflower, Sedum 'Autumn Joy', goldenrod, rudbeckia, shrimp plant, cigar plant, 'Indigo Spires' salvia, butterfly bush, Thunbergia grandiflora (sky vine), and *Salvia guaranitica*.

2

Landscape Design

Ideas for Getting the Most out of Your Landscape

A Landscape Should Fit Your Needs

Some people relax by working in their yard. Others hate yard work. Still others spend months travelling around the world and have no time for yard work. The same landscape will not fit the needs of all these people.

Home landscapes need to reflect the needs and desires of the homeowner. But, most homeowners end up with a landscape that is a reflection of everyone else's landscapes rather than a reflection of their own needs and desires.

It makes little sense today to not make better use of your landscape. Land is more expensive than ever. So you need to make the most of it. A good landscape plan helps you to do just that.

> **L**and is more expensive than ever. So, you need to make the most of it. A good landscape plan helps you to do just that.

A good landscape plan can pay off in financial terms when you sell your home, too. No one will dispute that an attractively landscaped home will attract more interest, and usually sell more quickly, than an identical house with a less attractive landscape.

Finding Help in Designing Your Landscape

So, you agree that it makes good sense to put a little extra thought, money, and effort into your landscape? But, if you're like most homeowners, you really don't feel competent at developing a landscape plan.

Contact several professional landscape designers or landscape architects. Find one that you like and with whom you'll feel comfortable working. Have them design a plan that you can either plant yourself or have a landscape contractor plant.

Don't trust all decisions to the landscape design professional. You don't call a building architect and simply say, "Design a house for me." Nor do you contact a real estate agent and say, "Pick out a house for me." You tell them what you expect. You read, learn about the choices, meet with the architect or agent on numerous occasions, and have continuous involvement in the selection process. The same must be true of a landscape design. No one cares about what you want as much as you do.

The sooner you involve a landscape design professional in the building process, the better. A good landscape design professional knows much more than a building architect or a building contractor about landscape considerations. A good landscape design professional can help prevent costly mistakes in tree protection, soil grading, house orientation, or other areas that crop up in the initial stages of home building or even smaller building projects. You might even consider involving a landscape design professional during the process of shopping for a home site. A good professional should be able to help you avoid buying a poorly drained site or other such problem site.

SELECTING A LANDSCAPE DESIGN PROFESSIONAL

How do you select a good landscape design professional? My advice would be to interview several. See what they know about local soil conditions, how to protect trees during construction, drainage, local plant materials, and landscaping for energy conservation. As you narrow your selection of a professional, ask to see other home landscapes they designed and had planted one to two years ago, and talk to the homeowners. Evaluate how well you communicate with the landscape design professional. If they don't understand you, or you don't understand them, there will be problems with the end result.

All this will take some effort. But you won't have to pay for this time. Later, once you're paying the professional for their time, you may wish you had spent more time at this stage.

You may wonder about the difference between "landscape designers" and "landscape architects". Laws vary from state to state. But, basically, landscape architects have completed a five or six-year degree in landscape architecture from a university. The course work is heavy in design. On the other hand, there are generally no training requirements for someone calling themselves a landscape designer.

This is not to say, however, that there are not experienced and talented landscape designers who will not do a better job for you than some landscape architects. The key to selection lies in the interview and investigative steps just outlined. Don't let your decision be swayed by low prices of an unqualified landscape designer. Likewise, don't be swayed by the high title of a landscape architect who doesn't know his local plant requirements and may draw a beautiful plan on paper that just doesn't work in real life. Interview, and talk to past clientele.

IF YOU DECIDE TO DESIGN YOUR LANDSCAPE YOURSELF

If you insist on doing the design work without the help of a landscape professional, do your homework. Use the plant lists in this book. Visit your local county Extension office to obtain reading material about plants suited for your area. Talk to reputable local nursery people. Ride through neighborhoods to spot landscapes that appeal to you. Take pictures. Talk to the people who care for the landscapes. Spend plenty of time planning your landscape before you start planting it.

Put your landscape plan on paper, drawn to scale. Otherwise, you will likely find that you will move plants a number of times trying to get the landscape to look just right.

Many nurseries will send a designer out to your house for a landscape consultation at an hourly rate. If you decide to plan the landscape yourself, I strongly urge you to take advantage of this modestly priced service before you start planting. A designer's second opinions may save you from some costly mistakes.

SOME PRACTICAL TRENDS YOU MAY WISH TO FOLLOW IN PLANNING YOUR LANDSCAPE

Smaller lawns. People are tiring of mowing large lawn areas that serve no functional purpose. Most people still want and need a lawn - for children to play, just for looks, whatever, - but they're making that lawn area smaller and more functional.

Retention of more natural areas in the landscape. What's the point of scraping an area clean of existing trees and brush with a bulldozer only to have to replant it, especially when that scraping process harms trees that you may wish to save? Progressive landscaping in areas such as Hilton Head, S.C. shows a definite trend toward retention of such natural areas in the landscape. If it doesn't need to be cleared with a bulldozer in order to place the house or plant a lawn, it's not.

Lots of small trees left on sites. The intense landscaping with lawn, foundation planting of shrubs, etc. is done close around the house. Further out from the house, and buffering the house from the street, remain natural tree areas with a forest floor. It makes for a very beautiful, serene, at harmony-with-nature landscape. Contrast this to the sterile landscapes that often result when everything is cleared and an acre of lawn grass is planted. Whereas the new trend of landscaping works with nature, the old method of landscaping struggles against nature.

Increased use of groundcovers. Whereas the

amount of space devoted to lawns in landscapes has been reduced, the amount of space devoted to groundcovers has been increased. People are discovering the advantages of groundcovers. They're easier to maintain than a lawn. And, they add a richness to the landscape with their varying textures. Also, as in the case of shaded areas, they'll often grow where lawn grass won't grow well. So, even though groundcovers are often more difficult to plant and establish, they're generally less demanding over the long run than is a lawn. Hence, the trend toward smaller lawn areas and larger groundcover areas has grown stronger.

Use of more color in the landscape. Ask any nursery operator and they'll tell you, color sells. Flower sales rise each year, as just about every homeowner plants at least a few flowers. But, not only are people planting more flowers, they're becoming more sophisticated in their use of flowers. They're using a wider range of annuals and perennials to extend flowering over most of the year. And, many people are carefully designing their flower beds with color schemes, flower heights, and foliage textures taken into consideration.

Color is provided not only from flowers, but from foliage colors and berries as well. People plant trees such as 'Bradford' pears because of their fall leaf color. Other plants, such as 'Savannah' hollies, are planted for their generous production of colorful berries. The 'Forest Pansy' redbud, a relatively new cultivar, is popular because of its red foliage in the spring and early summer.

Use of more drought-tolerant plants. Long periods of dry weather over recent years have made drought-tolerant plants more popular. Even homeowners with underground sprinkler systems prefer plants that don't require frequent watering.

Use of more native plants. Using native plants allows us to bring a touch of natural Florida into our own home landscapes. Donna Legare, co-owner of Native Nurseries in Tallahassee, says that she loves holly fern, an exotic fern, when she sees it in someone else's yard. But, inspired by what she sees in nature in Florida, she chooses Christmas fern and shield fern for her own yard. She bases much of her personal landscaping on the inspiration of nature, as do most native plant gardeners. Native plants must be placed in the proper habitat to grow well, though. They're no

different than exotic plants in that regard. Whether native or exotic, pick the right plant for a given site.

Use of more ornamental grasses. Pampas grass has been popular for some time. Recently, though, other ornamental grasses have been finding similar uses in the landscape. These other grasses are more versatile than pampas grass, though, because most are not as large as pampas grass. A wider range of foliage colors is available too.

Use of more trees. Ever since energy prices began rising, people have been more concerned with planting shade trees. During the 60's and early 70's, the lawn was probably considered the basis of most landscapes. Now, though, more and more people consider the trees the more important element of the landscape.

Use of improved cultivars of plants. With advances in plant breeding and plant propagation, a dogwood is no longer just a dogwood. People are learning the advantages of planting improved cultivars of dogwoods, such as 'Weaver', 'Barton', or 'Welch Junior Miss' over just planting a seedling dogwood. The same is true in the case of many other plants. Improved cultivars offer many advantages over seedling plants. An improved cultivar has been selected for some special characteristic and has been propagated to retain that characteristic uniformly from plant to plant. With seedlings, however, there is no uniformity. A seedling may or may not have the desired characteristics. There is much variability among seedlings.

Use of more mulched areas. Every square inch of the landscape does not have to be planted with lawn, shrubs, or flowers.

> *With advances in plant breeding and plant propagation, a dogwood is no longer just a dogwood. People are learning the advantages of planting improved cultivars of dogwoods, such as 'Weaver', 'Barton', or 'Welch Junior Miss' over just planting a seedling dogwood. The same is true in the case of many other plants. Improved cultivars offer many advantages over seedling plants.*

Some landscapes have large areas of mulched ground with no plants except the large trees above. This type of mulched area is especially common in yards that have plantings of pine trees. Rather than put so much effort into raking the pine straw each year, the homeowners let the layer of pine needle mulch accumulate to stabilize the soil.

Avoidance of pest-prone plants. Heavy reliance on pesticides in the landscape is out of favor today. Therefore, home gardeners tend not to select plants that they think will have many problems with insects, diseases, or other pests. For example, many home gardeners have opted not to plant hybrid tea roses, peach trees, or even gardenias because of certain pests which are common on these plants. Several retail nurseries no longer even sell redtop photinia because of a fungus leafspot disease that has become a serious redtop pest.

Water gardens. Many home landscapes now include some form of water garden. The sound of running water adds a soothing touch to the backyard landscape. And, as long as there is a shallow area in which they can stand, birds will often be attracted to the water. Small, relatively inexpensive recirculating pumps, pre-formed pool liners and an assortment of aquatic plants are readily available at many garden centers.

Landscape lighting. As we've become more sophisticated in our use of interesting plant forms, we've also become more creative in our use of landscape lighting. The landscape can take on a completely different character when illuminated by night lighting. Lighting the landscape at night extends the length of time in which we can enjoy the landscape. It also can serve as a crime deterrent.

Compost areas. Most of us like to do the environmentally correct thing, so we're beginning to make compost piles at home. It's not necessary that you have a fancy compost bin. What is necessary, though, is that you have an out-of-the-way place to pile the excess leaves, prunings, kitchen scraps (except meat), and other stuff that can be composted. This place needs to be close to a source of water (so it can be kept moist but not wet), and, if possible, should be in full sun. It also needs to be where you won't forget to turn it every couple of weeks with a fork. When the composted material begins to look like soil, you can use it to mix into flower beds, vegetable gardens, or other areas to be planted.

3

Soil Preparation

Successful Landscapes Build from the Ground Up

(Don't Skip This Section; You'll Be Sorry if You Do)

PREVENTING SOIL-RELATED PROBLEMS

It's an extremely common problem in some areas. A new house is built and the landscape is planted. But slowly certain types of plants die one by one. Even entire patches of the lawn may disappear.

Pulling up the dead plants, you may find that the soil is very moist. Sometimes water even stands in the planting holes.

Such soil is an adverse environment for many plants. Plants such as dogwoods, azaleas, junipers, boxwoods, and many other commonly used landscape plants just won't tolerate such conditions. The plant roots die from lack of oxygen in the water-logged soil. The top of the plant wilts and entire limbs may die and turn brown.

A common misconception is that low spots are the only areas with poor drainage. But, because there is little lateral drainage of water in the soil, even sides of slopes can be poorly drained.

Unfortunately, our landscape plans don't often include forethought as to soil preparation. If we took the time to plan ahead and include soil preparation as part of the landscaping process, adjustments could be made for such site conditions. But, as long as soil preparation is overlooked, we'll continue to have many dying shrubs and lawns.

HOW TO LANDSCAPE SITES WITH POORLY DRAINED SOILS

Before doing any planting in an area of suspected poor drainage, dig an 18-inch deep hole after you've had a good rain, preferably of an inch or more of rain. Fill the hole with water. If it takes more than several hours for the water to drain, then you should give careful consideration to drainage before planting.

If planned in time, there are several steps that can help in establishing a landscape on poorly drained soils. Raising the soil level is probably the most helpful of these steps.

Several feet of topsoil can be added to beds where you wish to plant shrubs and trees. Such mounded planting beds can be a tremendous help in providing adequate drainage during wet periods. Be sure that you mound entire beds, though, and not just individual trees or shrubs.

Even lawn planting sites can be raised by the addition of topsoil. When adding small amounts of soil (less than a foot) rototill the added soil into the existing soil. If the existing soil is compacted and heavy in clay, you may even first need to deeply cultivate it with a tractor-drawn bottom plow. Unless you mix the two soils together, you run the risk of having water perched above the old soil. Such a perched water table will cause serious problems for your lawn.

If you choose to use sand, it is especially

Unfortunately, our landscape plans don't often include forethought as to soil preparation. If we took the time to plan ahead and include soil preparation as part of the landscaping process, adjustments could be made for such site conditions. But, as long as soil preparation is overlooked, we'll continue to have many dying shrubs and lawns.

important that you mix the sand with the existing soil. Use sharp sand rather than a smooth, weathered sand. The jagged edges of sharp sand tend to create more pore spaces. Never use sand alone. Always use topsoil or some form of organic matter (ground pine bark, compost, etc.) with the sand.

When landscaping poorly drained or poorly aerated soils, it is important that you use plants tolerant of such conditions. Azaleas, junipers, dogwoods, boxwoods, redtops, and many other commonly used landscape plants just can't tolerate wet feet. Stick to plants, such as yaupon holly, ligustrum, wax myrtle, oleander, American holly, liriope, Asiatic jasmine, river birch, red maple, and other such plants that stand a chance of surviving poorly drained soils. For a more complete list of plants for wet sites, see the lists in the chapters on trees and shrubs.

EVEN DRIER SITES NEED SOIL PREPARATION

It is important to remember that plant roots need oxygen. Inadequate soil preparation is not just a problem in poorly drained soils. Even our common loamy soils are often inadequately prepared for plant growth. Trying to grow plants in soils on most building sites without rototilling or lots of shovel cultivation is the cause of many of the plant problems people encounter.

If you can't easily push a shovel into the soil, how do you think a plant will push its tender roots through such a soil? You must help the plant by breaking up a large area of soil before planting. Cultivated soil will be better aerated, better drained, and yet, better able to catch its share of rainwater before the water runs off the soil surface.

I recently looked at a planting for a commercial landscaper because he was having problems with some plants on the site. After being in the ground for a year or so, the plants were growing very slowly. The leaves showed some blighting and tip burn. Probing the ground with my shovel, I quickly found that soil right at the base of the plants was nice and workable. But, soil just a few inches out from the root ball was so hard that I really had to exert a lot of effort to drive the shovel into the soil.

The landscaper made the all too common mistake of not giving the plants good soil conditions under which to grow. A more thorough job of soil cultivation before planting would have given them a better beginning and would have resulted in much faster growth.

SHOULD YOU USE SOIL AMENDMENTS? (PEAT, COMPOST, ETC.)

For years it was recommended that you mix one part peat or compost with the backfill soil when planting a shrub or tree. Now university researchers have changed that recommendation.

Changing the soil composition of an individual planting hole creates a bath tub effect. During rainy weather, water from the adjacent soil will drain into the coarser-textured amended soil area and stand there around the plant roots. The oxygen in this waterlogged area will be limited. As a result, the plant roots will begin to die and the top of the plant will exhibit the symptoms as leaf margin burn or limb dieback, maybe even as complete plant death.

During dry weather, the amended soil in the planting hole tends to dry out quickly because it has larger pore spaces. So, the plant can suffer from drought stress even when the surrounding natural soil has plenty of moisture.

The current recommendation is not to use soil amendments in individual planting holes. If you wish to change the soil composition in a planting area that is poorly drained, compacted, or has extremely sandy soil, add the amendments to the whole planting bed and rototill them in. If you're planting an individual tree or shrub and wish to change the soil composition, create an amended planting bed large enough to accommodate future root expansion and plant the shrub or tree in the middle of the bed. Never just amend an individual planting hole.

Much of the time there is no need to use soil amendments at all, anyway. Pick a plant that can tolerate the type of soil on the site. Then take the time to thoroughly cultivate the soil for an area three to five times greater than the size of the root ball. The plant should grow well if it is given adequate care following planting.

It's when you try to plant a plant in soil unsuitable for that type of plant, or when you dig a planting hole little larger than the pot in which the plant was growing, that you'll have problems.

The Wrong Location Can Kill a Good Plant

Sometimes, even with reasonably good soil preparation, a plant just doesn't grow well. Provided it was a healthy plant in the beginning, it is probably just not suited to the site on which you planted it.

One lesson I've learned over the years is that if a certain type of plant doesn't grow well on a certain

Take time and forethought to match the plant to the site. Use the lists in the following chapters to pick the proper plant for the intended spot.

site, then it's foolish to keep trying to grow that plant there. Simply find another plant more suited to the site.

Plants differ in their tolerance to light levels, soil conditions, and other such factors. For example, some plants such as wax myrtles will tolerate the extremes of either dry sites or poorly drained sites. Other plants, such as azaleas will tolerate neither extreme.

Too often we put plants where they're really not happy. Dogwoods and azaleas, for example, don't like hot, dry sites. Other plants, such as crape myrtles or oleanders would tolerate hot, dry conditions much better.

Take time and forethought to match the plant to the site. Use the lists in the following chapters to pick the proper plant for the intended spot. I've tried to provide information to help make the job of finding plants for a given type of site a little easier.

Don't Neglect Plants Once They're Planted: Mulch, Water, and Fertilize— Properly

Once you put plants in the ground, don't leave them on their own. You'll need to mulch for a generous distance around them with pine straw, leaves, or other organic mulch. The mulch will conserve moisture, reduce weed competition, moderate soil temperatures, and provide some nutrients as it decomposes. Annually check the mulch. You should maintain it at about 2 inches deep. Don't let it get too shallow. But don't get it too thick either. Leave a space of 1-2 inches around the trunk free of mulch to prevent trunk rot.

Water the plants when needed, but water thoroughly and only when needed. At the first sign of drooping leaves, check the soil for dryness. If it's dry several inches deep, water. If it's still moist, don't water. Too much water can rot plant roots and starve them of oxygen.

When you water, don't just apply a little. It takes a lot of water to wet the entire root zone of a shrub or tree. You won't provide enough by standing there, spraying with the garden hose. If you're trying to do so, you're underwatering. You have to let the water run in one place long enough to

The current recommendation is not to use soil amendments in individual planting holes. If you wish to change the soil composition in a planting area that is poorly drained, compacted, or has extremely sandy soil, add the amendments to the whole planting bed and rototill them in. If you're planting an individual tree or shrub and wish to change the soil composition, create an amended planting bed large enough to accommodate future root expansion and plant the shrub or tree in the middle of the bed. Never just amend an individual planting hole.

thoroughly wet the soil four to six inches deep.

Don't water again until the soil dries out. A mulch, discussed earlier in this section, helps greatly in reducing the frequency of required waterings.

Water is needed year-round, not just during the spring and summer. Plants will use less water during the cooler seasons, and less water will be lost from the soil to evaporation then. But, there will still be times that the soil will become dry and you'll need to water during fall, and even during winter.

Supply added nutrients to the plants in terms of fertilizer. This is especially important in the early establishment years. Follow the fertilization recommendations given in this book in the chapters on various types of plants.

4

Plant Problems

Determining the Causes

THE MOST COMMON CAUSES OF PLANT PROBLEMS

When a plant is growing poorly, we tend to assume the problem is caused by some pest, such as an insect or disease. Usually, though, that's not the case. More often, plant decline is caused by the two factors discussed in the last chapter: either poor soil conditions, or trying to grow the plant in an unsuitable site for that particular plant.

Another common cause of plant decline is poor care. Is the plant base free of weeds and does it have a mulch around it? Do you periodically fertilize the plant, and do you water it when rainfall isn't adequate? Do you prune it with care, or do you haphazardly shear it without much thought as to where you're making the individual cuts? Remember, plants are living creatures. Neglect or abuse, in the form of competition from weeds, inadequate moisture or nutrition, and careless pruning or other types of wounds, take their toll on the health of plants.

So often such stresses weaken a plant and pave the way for the development of disease or insect problems. Just as when you or I get run down, sickness often follows. The same principle applies to plants.

So, when trying to diagnose a plant problem, first look for the obvious and the most common problems. Examine the growing conditions of the plant and the care the plant has received. Then look for the presence of insect pests, which you can often see. Finally, consider the possibility of a plant disease.

INSECT PESTS

Often with insect pests, you'll be able to see the culprit on the plant. Be careful, though, not to assume that just any insect you see on the plant is a pest. Some insects are not only harmless; they're actually beneficial in that they feed on pest insects. You certainly don't want to kill these good guys needlessly!

Basically, pest insects are of two types. There are the chewing insects, and there are the sucking insects.

CHEWING INSECTS
(CATERPILLARS, LEAFMINERS, BEETLES, AND SLUGS)

Damage of chewing insects is usually in the form of chewed holes in leaves. In the case of leafminers,

> *S*o, when trying to diagnose a plant problem, first look for the obvious and the most common problems. Examine the growing conditions of the plant and the care the plant has received. Then look for the presence of insect pests, which you can often see. Finally, consider the possibility of a plant disease.

the damage is in the form of chewed trails in the interior of the leaves, between the two surfaces of the leaf.

Not all insects chew. Only certain kinds, such as caterpillars and beetles, have mouthparts that facilitate chewing. Other insects, such as moths and butterflies, have harmless siphoning mouthparts which they use in gathering nectar from flowers. And, still other, such as aphids, have piercing-sucking mouthparts which they use to suck sap from plant parts.

It takes quite a bit of damage from chewing insects to cause significant harm to a plant. A few chewed leaves here and there isn't worth worrying about. However, if the damage is severe, insecticide control may be warranted.

Insecticide sprays are generally safer and more effective than dusts. Be sure to spray the undersides of the leaves as that's where the insects usually are found. Insecticides such as *Sevin®, diazinon, malathion, and Orthene®* are effective against many chewing insects. Be sure to read the insecticide label to ascertain that it's okay to use the spray on the type of plant you have and for the particular insect pest you have. Also, follow all the precautions and directions on the label for your safety and for effectiveness of the product.

Most chewing insect plant pests are *caterpillars*. *Bacillus thuringiensis* is the active ingredient in several insecticides that are very effective against most caterpillars. Dipel®, Thuricide®, and Biological Worm Spray are several possible tradenames of products containing BT. Use BT for caterpillar control whenever possible because it is not harmful to beneficial insects, to man, or to animals.

One unusual type of chewing insect is the *leafminer*. Called a leafminer because they mine or tunnel between the upper and lower leaf surfaces, they are the larvae of certain kinds of flies. The adult fly lays her eggs in the leaf and the hatched larvae

> **U**se BT for caterpillar control whenever possible because it is not harmful to beneficial insects, to man, or to animals.

spends its life tunneling between the surfaces. Other types of leafminers just leave blotches.

Leafminers are best controlled with a systemic insecticide such as Orthene®.

Systemic insecticides enter the plant's system rather than just staying on the leaf surfaces.

One type of chewing damage sometimes attributed to insects is not caused by an insect at all. *Slug* damage appears as chewed leaves, especially on tender flower plants or vegetable plants. But, you'll see no insect and won't see the slugs, either, because they feed at night. *Slug baits* are available from garden centers. The paste kind works very well, but be careful to read the directions and use only around plants specified on the label.

Beetles are another common type of chewing insect pest. Many beetles feed at night. If you note chewing damage on a shrub or tree, and you can find no chewing insect pest, it is a good possibility the damage was done by beetles.

BEETLES THAT BORE INTO TREES

Beetles that bore into trees usually only attack stressed or weak trees. The stress may be from such factors as drought, construction damage, or lightning. By the time beetles attack a tree, it is often so weakened that it would die even without the damage from the beetles.

The group of beetles known as the *pine bark beetles* operates in a similar manner. However, the pine trees these bark beetles attack, though stressed, would usually not die unless the beetles attack. Most pine bark beetles attack quickly and in large numbers. Often the trunk has many of the little balls of sap from the beetles' entry holes.

Once you note the signs of pine bark beetle attack, it will be difficult to save the tree by spraying. The beetles have already begun tunneling out beneath the bark, making egg-laying galleries. Soon there will be so many of these tunnels that the tree's circulatory system (located just beneath the bark) is disrupted and the needles of the tree will begin browning. At that point, it is definitely too late to save the tree.

Lindane and Dursban® are two sprays that can be used for pine bark beetles and other such boring insects. Follow the directions on the insecticide label. They are more useful as preventative sprays on the trunks of stressed trees than as curatives in trees that have already been attacked.

SUCKING INSECTS
(APHIDS, SCALES, LACEBUGS, MEALYBUGS, WHITEFLIES AND MITES)

The most common insect damage you'll encounter on plants is from sucking insects. Aphids, scale insects, lacebugs, and mealybugs, as well as mites (not really an insect), all have sucking mouthparts that they use to suck plant juices. The sucking of the plant sap results in various types of damage. Usually there is discoloration of the leaves. Often new growth is distorted and deformed.

Aphids (plant lice) are often seen clustered on new, tender leaves and stems. Aphids are most often light green, though some types are other colors. Often you'll see old, white shed skins around the pin-head size aphids. Another sign of the presence of aphids, whiteflies, or soft scales is the presence of sooty mold, a black film on the plant foliage. The sooty mold is a fungus that grows in the sweet juice excreted by these sucking insects as they feed. To rid a plant of sooty mold, you must simply bring the sucking insect problem under control.

Scales are usually found on the undersides of leaves or even on stems. Scales are insects with coverings, ranging from the appearance of tiny turtles (as with magnolia scale) to a sticky coating of snow (as with white peach scale). Scale insects really don't even look like insects because the insect is beneath a covering. Only when scales are young, before they form their coating, do they move around. Once their coating is formed they are stationary.

Mealybugs are closely related to scales. Instead of coverings, though, mealybugs excrete a white sticky coating in which they are free to move around. Mealybugs are white and have two tail-like appendages extending form their rear end. There are also small appendages around all sides of the mealybug's body.

Lacebugs, practically always found on the undersides of leaves, are common pests of azaleas and sycamores. Their damage is first noted as a speckling of the top of the leaf. Close inspection of the undersides of the leaves may reveal the tiny, lacy-winged insects or specks of their black, shiny excrement.

Whiteflies appear just as their name implies.

Certain plants such as gardenias and ligustrums are favored hosts. The adults don't feed, but the young, developing in small, round, flat cases on the undersides of the leaves, do feed. And, like aphids and soft scales, they excrete a sticky juice in which the black, sooty mold fungus likes to grow.

Mites are not insects. But their feeding damage is similar to that of sucking insects. Plant-parasitic mites are too small to be easily seen on a plant. The first sign of mite damage is usually a yellowish speckling on the upper surface of leaves. Also, on broadleaf plants, the new growth may be curled and distorted because of feeding during the development of the leaves. Webbing is sometimes evident with spider mites, especially if the mite population has reached high numbers.

One way to check for presence of mites is to rap the damaged plant parts onto a piece of white paper. If mites are present, you'll usually see them as tiny pin-point-sized dots crawling around on the paper.

INSECTICIDES FOR SUCKING INSECT CONTROL

Whenever you find damaging levels of sucking insect pests and have to use a pesticide, try to select the pesticide that poses the least risk to you and the environment.

Insecticidal oils are great for controlling many insects such as scales, aphids, whiteflies, mites, mealybugs, and lacebugs. Insecticidal oils generally are safer to the applicator and the environment than many traditional chemical insecticides. Some of the insecticidal oils that have been on the market for years specify on their label that the oil not be used when excessively high temperatures or freezing temperatures are expected.

New lighter insecticidal oil sprays are now on the market. These sprays should pose less risk of burning plants at high temperatures than previous formulations. High temperatures are usually interpreted as those over 85 degrees.

Year ago it was common practice to pour the dirty dishwater over the foliage of plants, such as gardenia, that had whiteflies or aphids. Soap is an effective and environmentally safe insecticide and can help control many insects, especially the sucking insects such as aphids or whiteflies.

Commercial soap insecticides, formulated specifically for safe use on plants, are available from most garden centers under tradenames such as Safer® Insecticidal Soap.

Be sure to follow all the directions and precautions on the soap formulation labels, though, just as if you were using any other pesticide.

*S*oap is an effective and environmentally safe insecticide.

When the soaps and oils don't work, you may have to resort to regular pesticides. Just use them carefully, according to label directions. And, except for rare cases such as when growing peaches or nectarines, don't use them preventatively. Normally, it's much wiser to wait until an insect problem develops before you spray.

Di-syston granules can be used for most sucking insects on many non-food landscape plants. Di-syston is a systemic insecticide that is absorbed into the system of the plant after being watered into the soil. Once in the system of the plant, it is ingested by the sucking insects when they feed.

Orthene®, a liquid insecticide, also has some systemic properties, and can be used for most of the sucking insects. *Diazinon®* and *malathion®* should also work on aphids, lacebugs, and whiteflies.

Never use an insecticide, or any pesticide, in a manner inconsistent with the label on the pesticide container. To do so can be a violation of Federal law and could be hazardous to your health. Only use the pesticide for the specified plants and pests.

PLANT DISEASES

Before jumping to the conclusion that an ailing plant has a disease, remember to first look for more common and obvious causes of decline such as poor drainage or compacted soil. Once you've eliminated such causes of decline and determined that there are no insect pests present, only then should you consider the possibility of a plant disease.

Most plant diseases are caused by one of three types of microscopic organisms: either plant-parasitic fungi, bacteria, or viruses. Fungus diseases are most common, followed by bacterial, and finally viral.

There are some chemical fungicides on the market that will help control certain fungus diseases, but there are very few bactericides and no viricides. And, a particular fungicide only controls certain fungus diseases. That's why it is important to correctly identify the specific disease.

Making chemical fungal disease control even more difficult is the fact that very few fungicides are systemic; they don't enter the system of the plant. Most fungicides work by providing a barrier on the plant surface that prohibits the germination of fungus spores and subsequent penetration into the plant. In other words, fungicides are primarily preventative agents, not curative agents. If most of the leaves of a plant already are infected with a fungus disease, then it is too late to spray. Spraying will only help prevent the infection of new growth and growth that is not already infected. Spraying is not a cure-all.

*T*here are some chemical fungicides on the market that will help control certain fungus diseases, but there are very few bactericides and no viricides. And, a particular fungicide only controls certain fungus diseases. That's why it is important to correctly identify the specific disease.

MAJOR GROUPS OF DISEASES

Stem Diebacks: The most common type of plant disease encountered is the stem dieback. With a dieback, tips of branches, entire branches, or even entire plants die. Dieback diseases, though, are not usually even actually true diseases. That is, the primary cause of the problem is not usually a fungus, bacterium, or virus. Most often, the problem can be traced back to poor soil conditions, poor care, or the plant being planted where it really doesn't belong. Pesticide sprays generally do no good for diebacks.

Sometimes diseases do cause diebacks. In such cases, pesticides still do little in controlling the problem because the disease organism is either in the vascular system of the plant or in the root system. The best thing to do is to *cut back the plant*, cutting into healthy tissue and removing the diseased portion.

When cutting back a diseased plant, you must be careful not to spread the disease organism from the diseased wood to healthy wood with your pruning tools. You will do just that unless you sterilize the pruning tools with alcohol or a 10% bleach in water solution between cuts.

Try to make your cuts six to eight inches below any signs of dieback. Examine the interior of the stem where you make the cut. If it is discolored, indicating disease activity, cut back several inches further. But, be sure to sterilize the pruning tools before making that last cut. Continue this procedure on each affected limb until you reach healthy wood.

Leafspots: There are many types of leaf spot diseases caused by a wide range of fungi and bacteria. Some, such as black spot on roses are so common that you may learn to identify them by sight. But most will require diagnosis by a trained person such as an experienced Extension horticulturist, nursery operator, or landscape pest control person. Or, they may even require laboratory diagnosis. See your local Extension agent to arrange laboratory diagnosis through your state university plant disease lab. You must *correctly identify* the leaf spot disease and causal fungus to know which fungicide to use.

*M*ost leaf spots on plants never develop to a serious enough degree to warrant applying fungicides.

Fungicide sprays will help with many leaf spot diseases if applied soon enough. But, don't wait until every leaf on the plant is severely affected and leaf drop has occurred before starting sprays.

On the other hand, don't become overly alarmed just because you see a few leaf spots on a plant. No plant is blemish-free, especially late in the summer. Most leafspots on plants never develop to a serious enough degree to warrant applying fungicides.

Consider the time of year, too. There's little to be gained in spraying a deciduous plant, such as a dogwood, in September, when it will be losing its leaves in a month or so anyway.

There aren't many cases where spraying of leaf spot diseases is really needed on ornamental landscape plants. Roses are an exception. Usually, if roses aren't sprayed on a regular schedule (usually weekly), black spot disease will eventually defoliate the plants.

Powdery mildew: Powdery mildew can be a significant leaf problem on some plants such as roses, crape myrtles, and euonymus. As its name implies, this fungal disease looks like a white powdery mildew growing on the leaves. The leaves soon yellow and fall. Fungicides such as Funginex® are available to control powdery mildew. Be sure the fungicide you select has the plant you wish to spray listed on the label.

Viruses can cause leaf problems, too. Again, the rose is a common host. Virus-infected rose plants usually have leaves with distinct bright yellow mottled patterns. There is **no chemical control** for viral diseases. Do not prune a virus-infected plant and then prune a healthy plant without sterilizing the pruning tools first. You'll spread the virus. Aphids can spread some viruses, too. It's advisable to remove virus-infected plants from plantings of roses.

Camellias sometimes get similar virus leaf mottling. Do not propagate from such infected plants and, again, be careful about spreading the virus by pruning. Otherwise, the virus on camellia doesn't seem to cause significant damage.

Azalea or camellia leaf galls are diseases that look worse than they are. Common especially during cool, rainy springs, these diseases cause thickened, distorted, and discolored leaves on azaleas or camellias. The affected leaves are quite shocking to most home gardeners, convinced their plant has some rare and terrible malady. Once you find the disease in the spring, the infection has already taken place and there's nothing you can do to remedy the situation. Nothing, that is, other than pick off all the affected leaves, put them in a garbage bag, and *get them out of the area so that they cannot provide inoculum for next year's infection.*

Azalea or camellia leaf galls don't kill the plants or cause any serious damage other than the only slightly unsightly presence of the deformed leaves.

Lichens: A lichen is gray or greenish fuzzy, crusty growth often found on the bark surface of many plants, especially declining plants. A lichen is a combination of a fungus and an algae. The fungus anchors the algae to the plant, and the algae, being a green plant, manufactures food for the two. Lichens are not parasitic to the plant on which they are found. They are only using it as a home. They would be just as happy on an old fence post or a wooden roof shingle, two other places they're commonly seen.

Unfortunately, because lichens are so often found on declining plants (probably because it's easier to become established on a plant that's growing and expanding so slowly), they're often blamed for the decline. Most often the decline is caused by poor growing conditions or poor care. Have the plants been fertilized and watered as needed? Are they mulched? Are they growing in an extremely sandy soil or in an extremely compacted soil or a poorly drained soil? The decline can usually be traced to such conditions.

No fungicide control is generally recommended for control of lichens.

MISCELLANEOUS PESTS

Moles: Moles are small, tunneling animals that make tunnels just beneath the soil surface in search of soil insects and earthworms. In the process, moles sometimes uproot small plants or cause uneven surfaces in lawns. Mole traps are available from many garden

Most often the decline is caused by poor growing conditions or poor care.

centers. Though difficult to catch, moles are not impossible to catch using such traps.

Don't waste your money on the poison baits sold for mole control. Moles only eat live insects or earthworms and such bait isn't attractive to the moles.

One or two moles, because of moles' wide-ranging activity, often give the impression that many moles are present in a yard and that a serious problem exists. Often, though, the few moles will soon leave an area for new feeding grounds and the problem will end quickly. So, considering the difficulty with which moles are trapped, patience is often the best remedy when moles are active in your yard.

Armadillos: Damage from armadillos digging in your yard may occur, especially if you live adjacent to

a wooded area. The armadillos are primarily nocturnal, so you may not see them. But, you may be troubled by the holes they leave behind in your yard as they dig for insects and worms.

As with moles, though, there is not an easy solution to stopping armadillos from digging in your yard. If you live out in the country where it's legal, you may resort to shooting them. You may also try trapping the armadillos in a live trap. But, then what do you do with an armadillo once you catch him? It is my understanding that the correct procedure is to humanely dispose of the armadillo. The armadillo being a non-native nuisance animal, your state Division of Wildlife prefers that you not release them where they will become a nuisance to someone else. So, only if the armadillos are causing a tremendous problem for you would you probably want to resort to trapping and disposing of them. The whole procedure could become rather involved and troublesome.

Deer: As our suburbs take over deer habitat, deer are becoming more and more of a garden pest. There are many home remedies: soap bars hung in plants; human hair hung in nylon stockings among plants; adding a beaten egg to a gallon of water and spraying it over the plants. One gardener even says used kitty litter spread around the affected plants works wonders - and really doesn't smell that bad once spread. There are commercial repellents such as Hinder that do seem to work but that require regular application. Nothing seems to work in all cases. Deer seem to have varying sensitivities to the various remedies. The only sure remedy seems to be a fence, 8-10 feet high, around the garden.

Deer also seem to have varying tastes as to what plants they will and will not eat. Deer in one area may not eat impatiens. But your deer may love them. Deers' taste will also vary with the season. They may turn up their noses at pittosporum this year, but next year when the woods are dry, your succulent pittosporum tips may be irresistible. So a good list of deer-resistant plants is all but impossible to develop. There always seem to be exceptions to the list. Still, the following may be worthy of consideration.

Trees: cedar, crape myrtle, cypress, dogwood, ginkgo, Gordonia, hawthorn, American holly, Jerusalem thorn, southern magnolia, red maple, oak, palms, persimmon, pine, redbud, river birch, or sweetgum.

Shrubs: Japanese anise, aucuba, banana shrub, barberry, boxwood, cherry laurel, elaeagnus, gardenia, cornuta holly, dwarf yaupon holly, juniper, leucothoe, ligustrum, mahonia, nandina, oleander, pyracantha, sago palm, viburnum, or wax myrtle.

Flowers: agapanthus, ageratum, bachelor's button or cornflower, butterfly bush, calendula, chrysanthemum, daffodil, gerbera daisy, iris, joepye weed, lantana, lobelia, marigold, narcissus, petunia, poppy, Goldsturm rudbeckia, snapdragon, spiderwort, vinca, or zinnia.

Groundcovers: ajuga, aspidistra, holly fern, ivy, Asiatic jasmine, Vinca major, or Vinca minor.

Vines: sweet autumn clematis or flowering jessamine.

Herbs: Most heavily scented herbs such as mint, Russian sage, lavender, rosemary, scented geraniums, or Mexican mint marigold.

Sapsuckers: Rings of holes in the trunk of a tree area a sign of feeding from sapsuckers, a type of bird. People often mistake the holes for insect damage. But, the straight lines of regularly spaced holes are characteristic of sapsuckers rather than insects. Unless the feeding is extremely heavy, though, over a long period of time, there is not significant damage. Temporarily wrapping the trunk of an affected tree with a material such as burlap may break the feeding habit on that tree.

Fire ants: Fire ants are more of a people problem than a plant problem. Fire ants, in case you haven't discovered the hard way, are the ants that make the large mounds and aggressively greet intruders with stings. Fire ants aren't especially large; they look like your typical ant. It's their habit of swarming in great numbers onto anything that disturbs their mound that makes them such a problem. Also, their large mounds can interfere with such routine operations as lawn mowing.

Several Fire ant baits (such as Amdro®, Logic®, and Affirm®) utilize the principle of worker ants taking poison bait back into the mound where the poison eventually is passed on to the queens. Such baits can be very effective though somewhat slow. Insecticide drenches (using insecticides labeled for fire ants) can also be used to kill fire ants. When using the drench method, you'll mix the appropriate amount of insecticide in the specified amount of water and slowly pour the mixture over the mound.

Insecticides simply sprayed on the mound surface, or contact-type insecticide granules (as opposed to baits), are not very effective controls. The key in fire ant control lies in getting the insecticide inside the mound and killing the queens.

Don't take your fight against fire ants too seriously. You'll never totally eradicate all fire ants from your yard for long, anyway. Just treat them one mound at a time as they trouble you. That way you'll keep the problem in hand.

Squirrels: "Tree rats" is a suitable term for squirrels. I've known squirrels to eat everything in the garden from tomatoes, to apples, to patches out of St. Augustine grass lawns. They can be a real nuisance.

Unfortunately, there is no known control for squirrels. In some cases, gardeners have caged them out of prized plantings with small mesh wire. In other cases I've known gardeners to keep the local population down with a pellet gun (this is a constant battle and I'm not sure about the legality). The bottom line is that there is no easy or very effective solution for the squirrel problem that so often exists in urban gardens.

Squirrels can be prevented from stealing pecans off pecan trees only if access to the tree is not available from adjacent trees or utility lines. A piece of smooth sheet metal or tin, wrapped around the trunk of the tree, about four feet off the ground, can prevent squirrels from climbing the trunk of a pecan tree. But, no limbs must hang low enough so the squirrels can reach the tree that way.

Birds: Birds can be pests of fruit crops such as figs, grapes, blueberries, or strawberries. Netting, to screen out birds, is available from many garden centers or mail-order catalogues. The netting is simply draped over the plant and secured at the corners. Sunlight can still reach the plant.

Yellowjackets: If you've ever stumbled into the underground nest of these yellow and black wasp or bee-like insects, you'll remember. When disturbed, yellowjackets swarm out of their underground nest in great numbers. And, because the nest is sometimes in an area in which you want to work or play, you may wish to destroy it.

Be careful! Many people are severely allergic to bee and wasp stings. If you're one of these, call on a pest control company to eradicate the nest.

If you wish to tackle the job yourself, scout out the area during daylight hours. Try to find all the entrance and exit holes to the nest. There may be several. Also, map out an escape route which will enable you to run away quickly without tripping.

Then plan to go back very late in the day when all the yellowjackets should be home and there's not much in and out activity. Dress as protectively as possible. Long sleeve coveralls are a great idea. Tightly secure cuffs with rubber bands to prevent yellowjackets from flying up sleeves or legs. A beekeeper's hat with veil would also be helpful.

You can use the hornet and wasp insecticides that come in an aerosol can (the kind that shoots a long, strong stream of insecticide with quick knockdown power). Or you can fill a pump-up sprayer with a mixture of an insecticide such as diazinon or malathion that is approved for control of wasps or bees. Direct a strong and constant stream of spray into the main hole and don't stop until activity from the yellowjackets ceases or until they start escaping and force you to retreat. Some people say they prefer using a drench rather than a spray. They simply pour their insecticide mixture into the hole rather than spray.

The key is simply to get a generous amount of insecticide mixture down into the nest without allowing the yellowjackets to get to you.

COMMON PESTS & POSSIBLE CONTROLS*

Pests	Possible Control
Azalea/Camellia leaf galls	Pruning out infected leaves and discarding.
Aphids/Whiteflies	Insecticidal soaps, insecticidal oils, malathion, diazinon, Orthene®, or Di-syston granules.
Beetles	Carbaryl (Sevin®), malathion, diazinon or Orthene®.
Caterpillars	*Bacillus thuringiensis* insecticides such as Dipel® or Thurcide®; carabyl (Sevin®); malathion; diazinon; or Orthene®.
Lacebugs	Insecticidal oils, insecticidal soaps, Orthene®, Di-syston granules.
Leafminers	Orthene® or Di-syston granules.
Leaf spot diseases	Fungicide depends on specific fungus.
Mites	Insecticidal oils or soaps.
Pine bark beetles	Lindane or Dursban® as preventatives only.
Powdery mildew	Funginex®, Bayleton®, etc. depending on the plant.
Scale insects/mealy bugs	Insecticidal oils, Orthene® or Di-syston granules.
Slugs	Slug paste or other slug baits.
Stem dieback/viruses	Pruning out the affected limbs to a point at least 6 inches below lowest symptoms of the stem. Sterilize pruning instruments in between cuts.

*Many of the pesticides specified here are for use on non-food plants only. Before using any pesticide, always read the pesticide label and follow the instructions and precautions carefully. Never use a pesticide in a manner contrary to that specified on the label. The label is the definitive authority. IF ANY INFORMATION IN THIS BOOK CONFLICTS WITH INFORMATION ON THE PESTICIDE LABEL, FOLLOW THE LABEL. ALWAYS TAKE THE TIME TO READ THE LABEL

Weed control using Glyphosate Herbicides. Glyphosate is the active ingredient in several herbicides that have been on the market for 10-15 years. Yet, many gardeners still don't take full advantage of these herbicides. The first release and best-known brand is Roundup®, but there are several other brands of glyphosate herbicides. They may vary in percentage of active ingredient, though, so always follow the label directions.

The beauty of glyphosate lies in its effectiveness and its safety.

Glyphosate is a systemic herbicide, meaning it is absorbed by green plant tissue (such as leaves or green stems) and translocated to the root system. Because of this mode of action, it doesn't kill upon contact. But, because it affects the root system, glyphosate is usually one of our most effective herbicides.

Glyphosate is a systemic herbicide, meaning it is absorbed by green plant tissue (such as leaves or green stems) and translocated to the root system.

Glyphosate is also fairly safe when used as directed. Its toxicity to you, the applicator, is not great. And, it does not remain viable in the soil. It is very quickly broken down by soil microorganisms.

There is one major precaution that must be heeded with glyphosate herbicides. In general, it will be absorbed by any green plant tissue. It doesn't distinguish between weeds and desirable plants. Therefore, you must allow no spray mist onto desirable plants.

Glyphosate will not be very effective on slick-leafed plants such as smilax or greenbriar. More of the spray runs off than penetrates. Repeat applications will be needed on plants with extensive or woody root systems.

All things considered, though, glyphosate can be a very helpful tool in the landscape. It can also be used for spot weeding in beds, between shrubs or beneath trees. If can be used for killing grass in cracks in walks or drives. It's very helpful in keeping grass away from young trees (just be sure not to spray the bark of young trees with green bark, such as peaches).

Glyphosate can even be used to edge beds.

Glyphosate is especially useful in killing grass and weeds in an area several weeks prior to being rototilled for a flower garden. You'll have less problems with weeds coming back after tilling if you'll spray with glyphosate first.

All you need for application is a small pump-up type sprayer (or even just a spray bottle for small jobs). For some jobs, you may wish to make a hand-shield of cardboard or plywood to keep the spray off desirable plants. The mouth of a plastic milk jug or a funnel, fastened upside down over the spray nozzle, may also help reduce spray drift if you lower the funnel to the ground over the weed to be sprayed.

Glyphosate is available in different concentrations under such tradenames as Roundup®, Kleenup®, Blot-Out® or others.

5
Trees

The Basis of a Comfortable Landscape

WHY TREES ARE SO IMPORTANT

We're all familiar with the benefits of the shade a nice shade tree casts. But, trees help on a global level by changing carbon dioxide into oxygen through photosynthesis.

The function of trees is more important than ever before because of the alarming rate with which carbon dioxide from the burning of fossil fuels is being trapped in our atmosphere. Scientists estimate that the level of atmospheric carbon dioxide could double in a few years if present trends continue. The rapid loss of our planet's forests to population growth worldwide has alarmed many scientists because of the significance in the global warming picture.

The buildup of carbon dioxide in our atmosphere prevents heat from escaping back into outer space. Some scientists say that the buildup of heat, sometimes called the greenhouse effect, will have a noticeable effect on the earth's climate within the next thirty to fifty years.

The experts disagree as to the degree of heat buildup. But even small changes may have great impact. The oceans will expand when heated, and the melting of the polar ice caps will further swell the oceans. Some experts say that since Florida averages about 15 feet above sea level, most of the state could be under water by the end of the next century. Worldwide, heavily populated cities such as New York, Boston, San Francisco, and Miami could very well be flooded. No one knows for sure if the effects will be so severe, but more subtle effects are almost certain to occur.

Present global temperatures are already the highest since records have been kept. The five hottest years of this century were in the 1980's. It wasn't just your imagination.

Though, as individuals, we may feel helpless in alleviating the greenhouse effect, we should remember the slogan, "Think globally, act locally." We can support the three R's (reduce, recycle, and reuse) to lower our dependence on fossil fuels. We can also help by doing our part to reforest our earth. Great strides are more often really the result of many small steps. Currently, only one tree is planted for every four that die or are removed in American cities and towns.

The American Forestry Association says that if current opportunities to improve tree growth were taken, the new growth would reduce atmospheric carbon dioxide by 450 million tons. That's about one quarter of the carbon dioxide the United States is estimated to release annually from burning fossil fuels.

USING TREES TO SHADE YOUR HOME

By strategically positioning trees to cast shade on windows, walls, and glaring surfaces around your home, you can also reduce your utility bill by 20 to

30%. Keep in mind, though, when deciding where to plant trees in your landscape that sun position changes with both the time of day and the season of the year. So, it is important that you take time to accurately plan where to plant your trees to shade the appropriate spot at the appropriate time.

In the early morning and late afternoon hours, the sun is low in the sky, and trees will cast long shadows. At noon, the sun is high in the sky, and trees will cast short shadows. So, if you're concerned with shading a portion of your home during the middle of the day, the tree must be close to the area to be shaded.

Shadows also change direction with the time of day. A tree casting shade on an object at 1:00 p.m. on a summer afternoon will not shade the same object at 3:00 p.m., or even at 2:00 p.m., unless it is a very wide tree planted very close to the object to be shaded. The sun travels a great arc in the summer sky and with each passing hour makes a great change in position in the sky. But, during winter the sun travels in a much shorter arc in the sky. There is not as great a change in the position of the sun from hour to hour in the winter sky.

What all this means is that in order to shade your home in the summer, trees must be positioned fairly close to the home and must provide a wide angle of coverage. You'll very likely find that it takes several trees to provide the same width of shade coverage during the summer that one tree can provide during the winter. If you plant trees during the winter (a good time to plant trees), keep these factors in mind.

PROTECTING EXISTING TREES DURING CONSTRUCTION AND LANDSCAPING

We spend a lot of time and money trying to establish trees in the landscape. And, we must wait years for newly planted trees to begin providing shade. It's a shame that we are so careless during construction projects with the trees we already have.

Though trees can be magnificent figures in the landscape, they also can be sensitive creatures. Too often we view them as simply structural components in the landscape, much the same as we view utility sheds, swimming pools, or other structures.

We need to realize, however, that trees are living organisms. Large trees took years to grow to their size. It takes years to grow a replacement. But it only takes minutes to cause irreversible damage to a tree.

We've made a lot of progress in getting people to realize that bulldozer scars (or, on a smaller scale, lawnmower scars) harm trees. But, it's more difficult to convince people of the spread of a tree's root system and of the importance of minimizing damage to the root system.

It's a common belief that tree roots extend outward only as far as the tree branches extend. Yet, research has shown *that tree roots often extend three times or more as far out as the tree branches extend.*

It's also a common belief that the shallow roots, those in the top foot or so of soil, are not vital to the health of the tree. But research has now shown that most of the roots that actually absorb nutrients, water, and oxygen are in the top two feet of soil. Furthermore, the roots in the top six inches of soil are much more important to the tree than ever thought before. Tap roots, those roots that extend downward like a large carrot, don't even exist in many cases. It's the shallower roots that really perform most of the functions so vital to the tree's health.

So, when shallow roots are scraped away during construction work, the tree suffers severely. Or, when six inches of clay fill is added over the delicate roots, restricting oxygen penetration, damage occurs. Even one pass of heavy equipment, such as a concrete truck, over tree roots can damage them. Roots are lost in all cases, and the loss can result in dieback in the tree's top.

So, when shallow roots are scraped away during construction work, the tree suffers severely. Or, when six inches of clay fill is added over the delicate roots, restricting oxygen penetration, damage occurs. Even one pass of heavy equipment, such as a concrete truck, over tree roots can damage them. Roots are lost in all cases, and the loss can result in dieback in the tree's top.

Home buyers often pick a certain home because of the trees on the lot. Knowing this, builders tend to leave a lot of trees on home lots. The problem is that they often abuse the trees during the construction process.

Very rarely do construction-damaged trees die before the home is sold. The home buyer buys a home with trees; they're just weakened trees. The trees may suffer a lot of limb dieback and limb drop in the following years. The trees often don't even totally die, at least not quickly. They just remain in a slow state of decline. The damaged, weak trees aren't nearly as attractive and full as they once were. Being weak, they're prone to insect or disease attack, or they may even blow over in a thunderstorm. Or, because of the weakened state of the trees, the homeowner is so afraid the trees may blow down that he pays a tree service to remove them.

EVALUATING TREE HEALTH AROUND NEW HOMES

If you're considering buying a new home with trees on the site, spend some time evaluating the health of the trees. A little investigating may reveal some potential problems.

Chances are that you didn't see the home during the construction phase. So you don't know what protection was provided the trees. Hopefully, there was minimal activity beneath the trees. Ideally, barricades should have been built out near the branch tips all the way around the trees. No clearing or construction activity should have taken place inside these barricades.

Most home builders don't build such barricades, however, so root damage to trees on home sites is very common. It's such root damage that usually leads to decline of the trees after the house is sold. It is important that you learn to detect signs of possible root damage.

If there's a lawn or cleared soil right up to the tree, you know that the soil was scraped. And, because so many tree roots are in the top six inches of soil, it is inevitable that some root damage occurred. It would have been much better if the natural leaf litter had been left around the tree and if the soil had not been scraped.

Whereas Northern cool-season lawn grasses will grow under trees, most Southern lawn grasses grow poorly under trees. Southern lawn grasses and trees just don't mix that well, not if you want to keep your trees healthy, have enough sun for the grass, and not have a maintenance nightmare mowing around trees. It's better to keep lawn areas open and let trees have the protection of their natural leaf litter as far out from their trunk as possible.

Environmentally-sensitive landscapes today retain some natural areas that a bulldozer has never touched. In such landscapes, the undergrowth was cleared away by hand or with the aid of glyphosate herbicides (such as Roundup®) without harm to the trees above. In some landscapes, much of the undergrowth is left for privacy screening. Wise home buyers are learning that using natural assets in a landscape is economically rewarding, too. Why scrape an area bare and then have to replant it?

If a tree is left sitting on a little mound of soil several inches above the surrounding soil level, you can tell that there has been considerable root damage during the clearing process. And, if you can determine that any soil has been added around the base of a tree, be assured that its roots have suffered. The degree of suffering depends on the amount of soil added. A couple of inches of sand fill may not be that harmful. But, six inches of topsoil fill would kill some trees, and several feet of topsoil fill would slowly kill most trees by suffocating their roots.

Not all home builders are careless about soil and tree management when building. But, home buyers need to beware of potential problems before they buy a new home. Large trees cannot be replaced and are very costly to remove.

DECIDING WHEN TO REMOVE TREES FROM YOUR LANDSCAPE

Trees are very definitely assets in the landscape. Trees cleanse and cool the air, utilize runoff water, stabilize the soil, provide homes for wildlife, and add to the property value of your home. Think long and hard before cutting them down.

Sometimes trees are removed for arbitrary reasons such as to give more light to grow a lawn or because someone is tired of raking leaves. Removing a large tree for such arbitrary reasons, though, needs to be considered a drastic step. There are alternatives.

Would it not be better to sacrifice a little lawn area and let the trees stay? And, rather than growing a lawn beneath the trees, why not just let the leaves accumulate to form a natural forest floor? You can control undergrowth if you wish with a couple of spot sprayings of glyphosate herbicide each year.

Trees require much less maintenance and energy inputs than does a lawn area. That's not to say that lawns don't still have their place. But, when water shortages and water pollution from runoff of lawn fertilizers and pesticides is a real problem, perhaps it is unethical to sacrifice healthy trees just because of the traditional American infatuation with estate-sized lawns.

Of course, there can be good reasons for removing trees, too. If a tree has suffered irreversible construction blight or other significant decline so that it poses a safety hazard, it needs to come down. Dead trees or trees with a large portion of dead limbs hanging over your house or driveway are candidates for removal.

But, don't be in such a rush to remove a dead tree on the back of your lot that doesn't present a safety hazard. Woodpeckers, nuthatches, owls, bluebirds, and other desirable wildlife use such dead trees for homes. If you remove dead trees that don't present a safety hazard, you're needlessly removing the homes for such desirable wildlife.

Don't be overly alarmed about trees with cavities in their trunk. A hole in a tree doesn't signify that the tree is not healthy. The part of the trunk that sustains life is on the outside, just beneath the bark. The cavity matters only in terms of structural strength. If the cavity consumes most of the trunk, then, possibly there is a safety hazard, depending on the tree's location. But a tree with a cavity only part of the way through the trunk of the tree may stand for another hundred years. Don't equate cavities with declining trees.

So, yes, there are times it is wise to remove trees. But, let's consider removal of large trees prudently. Even dead or declining trees can have value.

CONSIDERATIONS WHEN ADDING NEW TREES TO THE LANDSCAPE
(ESPECIALLY IF YOU DON'T LIKE RAKING LEAVES)

As mentioned already, lawns and trees just don't mix that well. So, when adding new trees to the landscape, if possible, try to keep the two separate. Otherwise, there will be several problems.

First, the grass will offer competition to the young tree. Recent research even indicates that grass releases substances that are toxic to other plants. Secondly, in your efforts to keep grass away from the young tree, you may bump it with a lawnmower or girdle it with a weed-eater. Such a wound can provide entry for disease organisms and be the start of decline for the tree.

Finally, if the tree does survive, as it becomes larger, it will cause problems for the lawn grass. We just don't have any southern lawn grasses that are really very shade tolerant. Some St. Augustine grasses, once well established, will tolerate moderate shade, but even they will not tolerate dense shade. And, as trees mature, the shade beneath them becomes more and more dense, making it more and more difficult to grow lawn grass beneath them.

One other advantage to keeping trees and lawns separate is that it can greatly reduce the amount of raking required in the fall and winter. Just let the leaves fall where they may. If you have existing trees in a lawn now, you may consider letting the area revert to its natural state for this reason alone, especially if the lawn grass is doing poorly in that area anyway.

The best approach is to plant your trees in beds rather than scatter them in the lawn area. The trend today is away from large lawn areas and toward larger natural areas and beds in the landscape. Lawn areas have become smaller and more functional. Natural areas, groundcover beds, and mass plantings of shrubs are in style because such plantings require less maintenance than open lawn areas.

RECOMMENDED TREES

The following are among trees recommended for our area. A short description follows each name. A distinction of which trees are native is not always made. Most of the trees are native, but non-natives

> The best approach is to plant your trees in beds rather than scatter them in the lawn area. The trend today is away from large lawn areas and toward larger natural areas and beds in the landscape.

included are considered worthy of planting also. The author feels that the important factor is selecting a tree suited for the intended site. Because sites to be landscaped are often no longer in their native condition, sometimes exotic plants are better suited than native plants. Some exotic species, though, are so aggressive as to crowd out native species. Such exotics, such as Chinese tallow, are not listed.

Following this list of Recommended Trees are further breakdowns of trees for special purposes. The descriptions of the trees in those lists can usually be found in this list of Recommended Trees.

SMALL TREES

Japanese maples (Acer palmatum): Various cultivars are available. Generally, slow-growing small trees noted for their twisted, Oriental style form and lacy foliage. Foliage, varying with cultivars, is red in spring and fall, some cultivars all season. Avoid dry sites and full sun.

Red buckeye (Aesculus pavia): Small native tree or large shrub. Needs a moist, fertile, good well-drained soil. Grows best in the shade of other trees. Showy red flowers in spring.

American hornbeam or blue beech (Carpinus caroliniana): Tolerant of all conditions except dry sites. Strong, attractive small native tree with smooth gray bark.

Redbud (Cercis canadensis): Early spring-flowering native tree with beautiful magenta flowers. Tolerant of dry sites and poor growing conditions.

Fringe tree (Chionanthus virginicus): A small, native deciduous tree that flowers in mid-spring with flossy, white clouds of flowers. Many birds eat the fruit that follows on the female plants.

Flowering dogwood (Cornus florida): Well-known but often mis-used small, spring-flowering native tree. Prefers good, fertile, moist, but well-drained site in the shade of other trees. Not best for street plantings and other hot, dry sites. Named cultivars, such as 'Weaver', 'Barton', etc. generally more showy than seedlings. 'Welch Junior Miss' is only pink dogwood for the Deep South.

Hawthorn (Crataegus spp.): Small spring-flowering native trees with white to pink flower clusters. Tolerant to wide range of soil conditions. Thorny branches. Leaves usually turn attractive red-orange in fall.

Loquat or Japanese plum (Eriobotrya japonica): Small evergreen tree tolerant of wide range of sites. If winter is mild during flowering stage, edible fruit may be produced in spring. Large, rich, dark green leaves.

Dahoon holly (Ilex cassine): Small to medium native evergreen holly tree. Will tolerate wet sites. Red berries in winter.

Deciduous holly or possumhaw (Ilex decidua): A small, deciduous native holly tolerating wet to dry sites. Spectacular show of berries after leaves drop.

Yaupon holly (Ilex vomitoria): Versatile small native tree or large shrub. Tolerant of wet to dry soils. Evergreen with attractive red berries on females. Very small leaves.

East Palatka holly (Ilex x 'East Palatka'): Hybrid pyramidal evergreen holly tree. One spine at tip of each leaf. Red fruit. Sun to shade. Tolerates wide range of soils.

Savannah holly (Ilex x 'Savannah'): Lots of red berries on pyramidal tree with dull green evergreen leaves. Tolerates wide range of soils. Sun to shade.

Crape myrtle (Lagerstroemia indica): Often pruned to limit size, will reach 25 ft. or more. Summer flowers of various pinks, reds, lavenders, and white. For sunny sites. Good fall leaf color. Attractive bark. Dry to wet sites. Use newer mildew resistant cultivars. Fast grower.

Ashe magnolia (Magnolia ashei): Small native tree or large shrub-type magnolia with very large, almost tropical-looking deciduous leaves. White showy flowers. Needs fertile, moist, well-drained site in shade of other trees. Keep mulched.

Southern crabapple (Malus angustifolia): Small native spring-flowering deciduous tree with pink flowers. Tolerates many soils but prefers fertile, moist, well-drained soil. Somewhat short-lived because of pests such as cedar apple rust.

Wax myrtle (Myrica cerifera): Large fast-growing native shrub or small tree; evergreen. Tolerant of wide range of sites from wet to dry. Females have gray berries that are attractive to birds.

Sourwood (Oxydendrum arboreum): Native tree that must have moist, fertile, well-drained soil. Beautiful red to purplish color in fall. White, fragrant, showy flowers in summer.

American hophornbeam (Ostrya virginiana): Native, preferring normal to dry sites, not wet sites.

Good urban tree, tolerant of adverse sites.

Jerusalem thorn (Parkinsonia aculeata): Small deciduous tree with very thin, almost fern-looking leaves. Bright yellow flowers in summer. Grows well in all soils except poorly drained ones. Branches have thorns, so either avoid planting in areas of heavy traffic or remove lower limbs below head height. Will be injured by severe freezes.

Chinese pistache (Pistacia chinensis): Tolerant of adverse, dry sites. Noted for spectacular fall color of red-orange. Not commonly used in the South, but worthy of trial here.

Chickasaw plum (Prunus angustifolia): Small native deciduous tree covered with clouds of white flowers in spring. Prefers moist but well-drained soils.

Cherry laurel (Prunus caroliniana): Large native shrub or small evergreen tree. Tolerates wide range of soil except the driest and wettest of sites. Birds will spread seeds and, therefore, can become somewhat weedy.

Taiwan cherry (Prunus serrulata): Small to medium size tree; blooming in very early spring or late winter. Very dark pink flowers. Seemingly the best Japanese flowering cherry for the Deep South. One of our earliest flowering trees.

Bradford pear (Pyrus calleryana): The most popular cultivar of the callery pear. Small deciduous ornamental tree owing most of its popularity to attractive orange to red-orange fall color. Also attractive white spring flowers when grown far enough north (Atlanta or so) and sometimes even further south after cold winters. Flowers followed by small fruit, not worthy of eating. Tolerant of wide range of soil conditions. Tough tree. Somewhat dense oval shape makes use as shade tree limited to small area beneath tree. Good tree for streetside plantings where uniformity is important and the dense, strong upright growth habit is wanted.

Chapman oak (Quercus chapmanii): Small deciduous oak native to our sandy, poor soils. Good for landscaping on such sites. Young growth is yellowish-green. Brown leaves stay on tree until following spring. Slow-growing.

Bluejack oak (Quercus incana): A tough, small deciduous oak native to dry, sandy soils. Young, unfolding leaves in spring are pinkish on top and silvery white on undersides, fuzzy on both sides.

Slow-growing.

Myrtle oak (Quercus myrtifolia): A small, slow-growing, evergreen native oak, very tolerant of dry sites. Common on coastal sand dunes. Small, rounded leaves with curled margins.

Coastal plain willow (Salix caroliniana): Fast-growing native evergreen willow for wet sites or good moist soils.

Tree sparkleberry (Vaccinium arboreum): Native, semi-evergreen tree with small white flowers in spring. For fertile, moist, but well-drained sites.

Chaste tree (Vitex agnus-castus): Attractive small deciduous tree with blue to purplish summer flowers, mildly fragrant. Fast-growing. Very adaptable to range of soil types and sites; tough tree. Foliage similar to marijuana.

Jujube (Ziziphus jujuba): Small date-like fruit bearing tree. Fruit ripens in late summer or fall. Tolerates dry sites but not wet sites. Deciduous.

MEDIUM TREES

Florida maple (Acer saccharum var. Floridanum or A. barbatum): The native sugar maple for the South. Great fall color, but dead leaves remain on tree in winter. Fairly tolerant of dry soils.

Red maple (Acer rubrum): Not tolerant of extremely dry sites, but great for most other sites. Red seeds in spring and beautiful red or yellow foliage in fall. Fast-growing native.

River birch (Betula nigra): Not tolerant of extremely dry sites, but an attractive multi-trunked tree for most other sites. White papery peeling bark is very attractive. Deciduous native.

Leyland cypress (Cupressocyparis leylandi): Tolerant of all but poorly drained or wet sites. Juniper-like evergreen foliage. Pyramidal, medium size.

Native persimmon (Diospyros virginiana): Tolerant of most sites except very poorly drained ones. The orange fruit is liked by wildlife, and once ripened by a fall frost, by many people. Fall webworms can be a problem for young trees.

Water ash (Fraxinus caroliniana): Native ash good for wet sites. Wood is light and weak. Rounded top.

Ginkgo (Ginkgo biloba): Very slow-growing medium to large deciduous tree noted for fan-shaped leaves that turn beautiful yellow in fall and drop almost uniformly. Prefers good sites.

Honey locust (Gleditsia triacanthos var. inermis): Thornless variety of our native honey locust. Very drought tolerant and tolerant of compacted urban conditions.

Loblolly bay (Gordonia lasianthus): Native broadleaf evergreen tree, native to swampy areas. Tolerant of wet sites. Showy and fragrant white flowers in summer.

Silverbell (Halesia carolina): Native, spring-flowering deciduous tree with white, drooping flowers. Needs fertile, moist, well-drained soil. Prefers growing in the shade of other trees.

American holly (Ilex opaca): Small to medium native evergreen holly. Prefers well-drained but not dry soil. Traditional holly leaves. Red berries on female plants.

Southern red cedar (Juniperus silicicola): Native needle-like leafed evergreen. Tolerant of all but wet sites. This and Juniperus virginiana are the cedars most of us know.

Goldenrain tree (Koelreuteria spp.): Small to medium deciduous tree with very showy yellow flowers in summer. Followed by showy brownish or salmon colored seed pods. Needs full sun to grow and flower well. Will tolerate dry sites but not poorly drained sites.

Japanese magnolia (Magnolia soulangiana): Small to medium tree with spectacular pink tulip or saucer-shaped flowers in late winter or early spring. Grow on good soils only, well-drained but not dry sites.

Sweetbay (Magnolia virginiana): Native evergreen magnolia tolerant of wet and poorly aerated soils. Leaves have silvery undersides. Showy, fragrant white flowers in early summer and at irregular intervals.

Water tupelo or black tupelo (Nyssa aquatica): Native tree, tolerating wet or good sites, but not dry sites. Good red or orange fall color.

Sand pine (Pinus clausa): Native pine, very tolerant of dry sites; not as large as most of the other pines. Needles are in bundles of two, about three inches long. Cones tend to persist on tree.

Spruce pine (Pinus glabra): One of the most attractive of the native pines; slender 3-inch needles, in bundles of two and attractive, shallowly furrowed bark. Retains limbs on lower part of tree, unlike most

southern pines. Useful for screening. Tolerant of wide range of soils. Not as tall as most native pines.

Sawtooth oak (Quercus acutissima): Very tough oak, good for most any type of site. Fall color is brown; brown leaves persist into winter. Sawtoothed leaves. Native to Korea, China, and Japan.

Bluff oak (Quercus austrina): Native deciduous oak with large, white oak-like leaves. For fertile, moist, but well-drained soils. Attractive shaggy bark that flakes into long strips.

Turkey oak (Quercus laevis): Native oak very tolerant of dry sites. Large, deeply cut leaves turn brilliant red in fall, then remain brown on tree until next spring.

Blackjack oak (Quercus marilandica): Native, deciduous oak with large paddle-shaped leaves which hang on the tree after browning. Not readily available in nurseries, but is tough, durable tree, tolerant of dry sites.

Chinquapin oak (Quercus muehlenbergii): Native, though not common, deciduous oak with large sharp-toothed leaves. Tolerant of most sites except compacted clays or wet sites. Sometimes good fall color.

Post oak (Quercus stellata): Native deciduous oak very tolerant of dry and adverse conditions. However, existing older trees will not tolerate much abuse in way of root damage or compaction. Has broad lobed leaves with somewhat flat end on middle lobe. Difficult to transplant, so not readily available in nurseries.

Sassafras (Sassafras albidum): Not for extremely dry sites. Otherwise, good fast-growing native tree. Excellent fall color. Difficult to transplant; difficult to find in nurseries. Leaves can be oval-shaped or have one, two, or three lobes, all on same tree.

Basswood (Tilia floridana, T. caroliniana): Natives for fertile, moist, but well-drained sites. Deciduous, rounded leaves with single point at end. Inconspicuous flowers very attractive to bees. *T. floridana* larger than *T. caroliniana*.

Winged elm (Ulmus alata): Very tough, drought tolerant, native elm. Would make an excellent street tree. Has corky, winged bark.

Florida elm (Ulmus americana floridana): Is a native form of the American elm. Not for dry or poor sites. Smooth, wingless twigs as opposed to winged elm.

Lacebark elm or Chinese elm (Ulmus parvifolia): Excellent moderately-sized shade tree, very popular because of fast growth rate, attractive bark, attractive weeping growth habit, and tolerance of wide range of extreme sites, including very dry sites and compacted soils. 'Drake' is popular cultivar. Should not be shunned because of being a non-native.

LARGE TREES

Hickory (Carya spp.): Several species exist as native trees. Difficulty in transplanting prohibits wide nursery production. Worthy of protecting existing trees on sites, though, for beautiful yellow fall color. Very sensitive to root disturbance. Pignut hickory, *C. glabra*, has drought tolerance.

Deodar cedar (Cedrus deodara): Tolerant of all but poorly drained soils. Pyramidal, silvery-blue needle evergreen tree. Medium size. Native to Himalayan Mountains, but grows rapidly here under good growing conditions.

Sugarberry (Celtis laevigata): Deciduous native with smooth bark except for prominent corky warts. Bears orange-red berries which attract birds. Best for fertile, moist soils.

American beech (Fagus grandifolia): A magnificent native tree, but a slow grower. Needs fertile, well-drained but moist woodlands type soil. Grass competition is detrimental. Beautiful smooth bark. Gold leaves in fall, persist as brown leaves in winter. Protect at all costs when existing on sites.

White ash (Fraxinus americana): Good native shade tree for sites with fertile, moist, but well-drained soil. Not for compacted soils. Will tolerate some wetness if not too heavy clay. Yellow to yellow-orange in fall.

Green ash (Fraxinus pennsylvanica): More tolerant of adverse sites than white ash, but neither is good on heavy clay soils. Faster grower than white ash. Typically has seven leaflets per leaf whereas white ash has nine or more.

Sweetgum (Liquidambar styraciflua): Native with strong upright growth habit as opposed to spreading crown. Not for extremely dry sites. Spiny burs can be nuisance in a lawn. Excellent yellow to red-orange fall color.

Tulip poplar or yellow poplar (Liriodendron tulipifera): Huge native tree needing large area. Not for dry sites or compacted soils. Somewhat brittle wood. Leaves drop sporadically throughout the season.

Southern magnolia (Magnolia grandiflora): Stately native broadleaf evergreen tree. Doesn't tolerate dry conditions. Does not tolerate root disturbance. Best to leave low branches on tree to hide fallen leaves and protect against root damage. Beautiful fragrant white flowers in spring to mid-summer. Cone-shaped fruits ripen to expose red seeds in late summer to fall. Several improved cultivars available. Sensitive to magnesium deficiency, so young trees may benefit from applications of Epsom salts.

Black gum (Nyssa sylvatica): Native for wet to only moderately dry sites. Beautiful red or red-orange fall foliage.

Shortleaf pine (Pinus echinata): Native pine, tolerant of all soil types but the poorest drained of soils. Fast-growing, attractive pine with 3-5 inch needles, usually in bundles of two. Very small cones.

Slash pine (Pinus elliotti): Native pine with long, 7-12 inch needles in bundles of two or three. Tolerates wet soils. Fast grower.

Longleaf pine (Pinus palustris): Native pine with long, 8-10 inch needles in bundles of three. Cones are very large, 6-10 inches long. Tolerates dry soils. Slow growing the first few years.

Pondpine (Pinus serotina): Native pine tolerant of high or fluctuating water levels. 6-11 inch needles in bundles of three, sometimes four. Cones are more rounded than those of most pines. Branches lower on trunk than most pines.

Loblolly pine (Pinus taeda): Native pine that will tolerate poorly drained soils, though will tolerate mildly dry conditions, too. Needles are 6-9 inches long, in bundles of three.

Sycamore (Platanus occidentalis): Huge native tree, requiring lots of room. Use only on large sites. Dieback disease and lacebugs can be a problem. Some people don't like the cleanup of the large deciduous leaves.

White oak (Quercus alba): Long-lived, native oak with moderate growth rate, eventually becoming a stately tree. Large lobed leaves, sometimes turning dark red or orange-red in fall. Not for dry sites or compacted soils.

Southern red oak (Quercus falcata): Native oak tolerant of both dry and poorly drained soils. Fast grower. Fall color is usually just brown or yellow-brown.

Laurel oak (Quercus laurifolia): Native evergreen oak tolerant of wide range of soil conditions. Like water oak, not relatively long-lived and somewhat spindly shape.

Swamp chestnut oak (Quercus michauxii): Deciduous oak native to good, fertile sites; not for dry sites. attractive large chestnut-like leaves and large acorns.

Water oak (Quercus nigra): Fast-growing, large, semi-evergreen, native oak. Tolerant of wet sites and compacted soils. Not a highly desirable tree for planting, though, because of relatively short life span and somewhat spindly growth habit on many sites. May be worth saving when existing on sites, though. Leaves are somewhat paddle-shaped. No attractive fall color.

Willow oak (Quercus phellos): Deciduous oak with thin, willow-like leaves. Will not tolerate dry soils. Native to rich bottomlands.

Shumard oak (Quercus shumardii): A native deciduous oak that should be planted more. Tolerant of wide range of soil conditions. Beautiful red to orange fall foliage. Large pointed red-oak type leaves.

Live oak (Quercus virginiana): The magnificent native evergreen oak so popular in the Deep South. Tolerant of wide range of soil conditions. There are various varieties or subspecies that have evolved. So, leaf size, form, and growth habit may vary considerably among live oaks.

Bald cypress and pond cypress (Taxodium spp.): Deciduous native cypresses that will tolerate but don't require excessive moisture. Because of tolerance for poor aeration, will tolerate compacted, urban soils quite well. Will not tolerate extremely dry sites, though. Beautiful, lacy foliage that turns bronze in fall.

Good Fast-Growing Shade Trees

Florida maple (*Acer floridanum* or *A. barbatum*)
Red maple (*Acer rubrum*)
River birch (*Betula nigra*)
Sugarberry (*Celtis laevigata*)
Sweetgum (*Liquidambar styraciflua*)
Tulip poplar (*Liriodendron tulipifera*)
Sycamore (*Platanus occidentalis*)
Sawtooth oak (*Quercus acutissima*)

Laurel oak (*Quercus laurifolia*)
Water oak (*Quercus nigra*)
Sassafras (*Sassafras albidum*)
Chinese, Lacebark, or Drake elm (*Ulmus parvifolia* 'Drake')

Trees Tolerant of Dry Sites

Sugarberry (*Celtis laevigata*)
Redbud (*Cercis canadensis*)
Leyland cypress (*Cupressocyparis leylandi*)
Native persimmon (*Diospyros virginiana*)
Honey locust (*Gleditsia triacanthos var. inermis*)
Red cedar (*Juniperus virginiana*)
Goldenrain tree (*Koelreuteria spp.*)
Wax myrtle (*Myrica cerifera*)
Jerusalem thorn (*Parkinsonia aculeata*)
Sand pine (*Pinus clausa*)
Longleaf pine (*Pinus palustris*)
Chinese pistache (*Pistacia chinensis*)
Chickasaw plum (*Prunus angustifolia*)
Sawtooth oak (*Quercus acutissima*)
Bluejack oak (*Quercus incana*)
Turkey oak (*Quercus laevis*)
Chinquapin oak (*Quercus muehlenbergii*)
Myrtle oak (*Quercus myrtifolia*)
Post oak (*Quercus stellata*)
Live oak (*Quercus virginiana*)
Cypress (*Taxodium spp.*)
Winged elm (*Ulmus alata*)
Lacebark elm (*Ulmus parvifolia*)
Chaste tree (*Vitex agnus-castus*)
Jujube (*Ziziphus jujuba*)

Trees Tolerant of Wet Sites

Red maple (*Acer rubrum*)
River birch (*Betula nigra*)
American hornbeam or blue beach (*Carpinus caroliniana*)
Loblolly bay (*Gordonia Iasianthus*)
Dahoon holly (*Ilex cassine*)
Sweetgum (*Liquidambar styraciflua*)
Tulip poplar (*Liriodendron tulipifera*)
Wax myrtle (*Myrica cerifera*)
Southern magnolia (*Magnolia grandiflora*)
Sweetbay (*Magnolia virginiana*)
Water tupelo (*Nyssa aquatica*)
Black gun (*Nyssa sylvatica*)
Slash pine (*Pinus elliotti*)

Spruce pine (*Pinus glabra*)
Pond pine (*Pinus serotina*)
Loblolly pine (*Pinus taeda*)
Sycamore (*Platanus occidentalis*)
Willow oak (*Quercus phellos*)
Shumard oak (*Quercus shumardii*)
Live oak (*Quercus virginiana*)
Sabal or cabbage palm (*Sabal palmetto*)
Weeping willow (*Salix babylonica*)
Coastal plain willow (*Salix caroliniana*)
Bald cypress and pond cypress (*Taxodium spp.*)

EVERGREEN TREES

Deodar cedar (*Cedrus deodora*)
Leyland cypress (*Cupressocyparis leylandi*)
Loquat (*Eriobotrya japonica*)
Loblolly bay (*Gordonia lasianthus*)
Dahoon holly (*Ilex cassine*)
American holly (*Ilex opaca*)
Yaupon holly (*Ilex vomitoria*)
Red cedar (*Juniperus virginiana*)
Wax myrtle (*Myrica cerifera*)
Southern magnolia (*Magnolia grandiflora*)
Sweetbay (*Magnolia virginiana*)
Sand pine (*Pinus clausa*)
Slash pine (*Pinus elliotti*)
Spruce pine (*Pinus glabra*)
Longleaf pine (*Pinus palustris*)
Pond pine (*Pinus serotina*)
Loblolly pine (*Pinus taeda*)
Cherry laurel (*Prunus caroliniana*)
Laurel oak (*Quercus Iaurifolia*)
Myrtle oak (*Quercus myrtifolia*)
Live oak (*Quercus virginiana*)

PALMS

Pindo palm (Butia capitata): Medium, 10-20 ft., palm with gray-green feathery leaves. Tolerant of wide range of soil types and sites. Produces orange edible fruit, normally used in jellies rather than eaten fresh.

European fan palm (Chamaerops humilis): Small, 6-8 ft. palm that tolerates wide range of soil conditions. Salt-tolerant. Fan-shaped leaves. Slow-growing.

Canary Island date palm (Phoenix canariensis): Large, 30-60 ft. stocky palm with feathery leaves. Not as tolerant of poor soils, especially poorly drained soils, as other palms. So large as to be out of scale with most homes.

Needle palm (Rhapidophyllum hystrix): Small, 3-5 ft. native palm that prefers fertile, moist soils and a little shade. Needle-like spines at the base. Extremely cold-hardy.

Sabal palm or cabbage palm (Sabal palmetto): Tall, 30-60 ft., slender native palm. Tolerates wide range of soil conditions once established. Fan-shaped leaves twisting on the stem.

Windmill palm (Trachycarpus fortunei): Slow-growing to 10-15 ft. Tolerant of many soils, but does best in a well-drained one. Very showy, fan-shaped leaves. Trunk is wrapped in a blackish, hair-like fiber. Tolerates moderate shade and low temperatures.

Mexican Washington palm (Washingtonia robusta): Very tall, 60-80 ft., slender palm. Old leaves hang down the trunk just beneath the green fan-shaped foliage. Tolerant of wide range of soil types.

FERTILIZATION OF TREES

Don't over-fertilize trees. Small and recently planted trees only several feet tall would require no more than about four tablespoons of a 16-4-8 or 12-4-8 fertilizer. Apply this in early March and then again in July. Spread the fertilizer on the soil surface extending out slightly beyond the branch tips of the tree. There's no need to remove mulch before spreading the fertilizer; just apply it over the top of the mulch and water it in.

For larger trees, apply one cup of the fertilizer per inch of trunk diameter as measured 4 feet above the ground. Apply in March and again in July. If you use an 8-8-8 or 10-10-10 fertilizer, increase the rate by one-third. Spread the fertilizer over the root zone of the tree, starting several feet out from the trunk and extending beyond the branch tips of the tree. In fact, about ⅓ of the fertilizer should be applied beyond the branch tips as many of the roots will be in that area.

An even better method of fertilization is to apply the same total amount of fertilizer, but apply smaller amounts more often. Using this method, more of the fertilizer would be used by the tree and less would be wasted.

Reduce the fertilizer rates on older trees with trunk diameters over 12 inches (as measured 4 ft. above the ground). Accelerated growth rates are usually not desired on these trees, so they don't need as much fertilizer. Stop fertilizing the tree when it reaches the desired size. In fact, if you pick the right tree for a site, and if the leaf litter is allowed to decompose at the base of the tree, it can get by with no supplemental fertilization for most of its life.

FLOWERING TREES

SEQUENCE OF BLOOM	FLOWER COLOR	NORMAL TIME OF YEAR
Flowering cherries	Pinks, rose	Early-mid February
Japanese magnolias	White, pink, purple	Early-mid February
Red maple	Rusty red	Mid-late February
Redbud	Lavender, pinks	Mid-late February
Red buckeye	Red	Late February-early March
Chickasaw plum	White	Late February-early March
Crabapple	Pink	Early March
Flowering dogwood	White	Early-mid March
'Welch Jr. Miss' dogwood	Pink	Early-mid March
Silverbell	White	Mid March-early April
Hawthorns	White	Mid March-early April
Tree sparkleberry	White	Mid March-early April
Fringetree	White	Early-mid April
Ashe magnolia	White	May
Jerusalem thorn	Yellow	May-September
Mimosa	Pink	May-August
Southern magnolia	White	June
Goldenrain tree	Yellow	June
Sourwood	White	June
Chaste tree	Blue-purple	July-August
Crape myrtle	White, pink, lavender, red	June-September

TREES WITH ATTRACTIVE LEAF COLOR

TREE	COLOR	TIME OF YEAR
American beech	Golden bronze	Fall
Bald or pond cypress	Russet-orange	Fall
Black gum	Orange to red	Fall
Bradford pear	Red-orange	Fall
Chinese pistache	Red-orange	Fall
Crape myrtle	Red, red-orange	Fall
Dogwood	Red, purplish red	Fall
Florida maple	Red-orange	Fall
Ginkgo	Bright yellow-gold	Fall
Hickory	Yellow	Fall
Japanese maples	Red, orange-red, purple	Spring, summer &/or fall

Red maple	Yellow, scarlet red	Fall
Redbud	Yellow	Fall
Sassafras	Orange to red-orange	Fall
Sawtooth oak	Golden brown	Fall
Shumard oak	Red-orange	Fall
Sourwood	Red	Fall
Sweetgum	Yellow, orange, purple	Fall
Tulip poplar	Yellow	Fall
Water tupelo	Orange to red	Fall
White oak	Red, orange	Fall
Willow oak	Pale yellow	Fall
Winged elm	Pale yellow	Fall

TREES WITH OTHER ATTRACTIVE FEATURES

TREE	ATTRACTIVE FEATURE
American holly	Red berries
Chaste tree	Leaf shape
Chinese pistache	Fruit
Crape myrtle	Attractive bark and form
Deciduous holly (possumhaw)	Bright red berries
Flowering dogwood	Red fruit, nice shape
Ginkgo	Unique leaf shape
Goldenrain tree	Pink fruit pods
Japanese maples	Leaf shape and branch form
Lacebark elm	Peeling bark
Loquat	Edible fruit, fragrant flowers
Red maple	Showy fruit in early spring
River birch	Peeling bark
Yaupon holly	Red berries
Southern magnolia	Fruit
Sycamore	White bark
Jujube (*Ziziphus jujuba*)	Sweet, edible date-like fruit

The roots of trees often extend outwards three times or more as far as the top branches extend. And, many of the important roots are in the top two feet of soil. In fact, the roots in the top six inches of soil are much more important than commonly thought. Considerable damage is often done to these shallow roots unless precautions are taken when working around trees.

6
Shrubs

Selecting the Right Ones for the Site

Shrubs are used in the landscape for various purposes. They are used around the foundation of the house to hide less-than-attractive architectural features and to enhance the appearance of the house. They are used in hedges to screen views. Shrub plantings are also useful in providing habitats and food for birds and other desirable wildlife. Sometimes shrubs are used just because they're especially attractive, fragrant, or have some other desirable characteristic.

Just as there are numerous reasons for planting shrubs, there are numerous types of shrubs that you can plant. However, not all will perform any one function and not all will grow well on all sites. Some shrubs, because of their height, are better for planting around a house's foundation or under windows than other shrubs. These same shrubs, though, probably wouldn't make a good screening hedge.

Some shrubs will tolerate wet, poorly drained soils. Others will tolerate dry soils and full sun. Some shrubs that you may have grown in another part of the country may not even grow here.

It is important to select the right shrub for a given site and given use. Proper selection will save you many hours of headaches and maintenance for years after planting. The following lists were compiled to help you in your selection.

Of course, it's helpful to know what the plants on the list look like. So, use these lists in conjunction with a trip to your favorite nursery.

> *I*t is important to select the right shrub for a given site and given use. Proper selection will save you many hours of headaches and maintenance for years after planting.

SMALL SHRUBS
(NORMALLY LESS THAN 4 FT.)

Sherwood abelia (Abelia grandiflora 'Sherwoodii'): Dwarf form of abelia, an old summer-flowering favorite. White flowers, glossy leaves. Sun to light shade. Prefers fertile, moist soil.

Ardisia (Ardisia crenata): Small shade plant, glossy leaves, red berries. For good fertile sites. Is a good choice for shaded, informal landscapes. Birds will spread the seeds. Hardy to the mid teens.

Crimson pygmy barberry (Berberis thunbergii 'Atropurpurea Nana'): Deciduous, red foliage. For sunny, well-drained sites.

Japanese boxwood (Buxus microphylla): Small evergreen leaves. Sun to shade. Not for extremely dry or poorly drained soils. Occasional problems with mites or nematodes. But, overall, is still a very low maintenance shrub.

Creeping euonymus (Euonymus fortunei): Evergreen, most cultivars variegated. Almost a ground cover. Sun to light shade. Tolerates a wide range of soil types. Green cultivars turn rich burgundy in winter.

Prostrate gardenia (Gardenia jasminoides 'Radicans'): Miniature version of the evergreen shrub gardenia. White fragrant flowers. Very susceptible to whiteflies and nematodes. Short-lived. Prefers fairly good soil.

Carissa holly (Ilex cornuta 'Carissa'): Attractive small evergreen holly for sun to partial shade. Each leaf has one spine. Few if any berries. Tolerates all but the driest and the wettest of soils. Practically no pruning needed.

Dwarf Chinese holly (Ilex cornuta 'Rotunda'): Compact, dense, evergreen holly for sun to shade. Practically no pruning needed. Very good plant for wide range of sites. Interesting, coarse texture due to spiny leaves.

Dwarf yaupon holly (Ilex vomitoria 'Nana'): This is a dwarf form of the very versatile native yaupon. Other dwarf cultivars include 'Stokes Dwarf' and 'Schillings'. Tolerant of wide range of soil conditions and sun to shade. No berries on the dwarf forms, but they serve as pollinators for other berry-producing hollies. Practically no pruning needed. Very good plant.

Compact Pfitzer (Juniperus chinensis 'Pfitzer Compact'): Smaller version of the Pfitzer juniper, only reaching 3-4 ft. high and 6-8 ft. wide. For full sun. Will tolerate dry sites but not wet sites.

Shore juniper (Juniperus conferta): Grows to 2-3 ft. tall, good for mass planting as ground cover in full sun or light shade. Will tolerate all sites except wet, poorly drained ones. 'Blue Pacific' is a more compact, neater cultivar for most home landscapes.

Parsoni juniper (Juniperus davurica): One of the best low-growing junipers. For full sun to light shade. Feathery foliage. To about 2 ft. tall. Not for poorly drained soil.

Spreading juniper (Juniperus horizontalis): There are several cultivars, including 'Bar Harbor' or 'Blue Rug', which grow to 6-8 inches, and 'Plumosa' or Andorra, which grow to 1-2 ft. Are a ground cover type planting for full sun or light shade. Prefers dry conditions.

Dwarf crape myrtle (Lagerstroemia indica): Deciduous, flowering, full sun. Tolerates wide range of soil conditions.

Dwarf nandina (Nandina domestica): There are many cultivars of dwarf nandinas such as 'Compacta', 'Nana', 'Harbour Dwarf', etc. Some have excellent fall and winter red color. For sun to shade and tolerant of wide range of soil conditions. Give a soft, natural look to the landscape.

Wheeler's Dwarf pittosporum (Pittosporum tobira 'Wheeler's Dwarf'): Excellent evergreen, compact plant for sun to shade. Practically no pruning needed. Will grow on wide range of sites. Stems are very brittle, so avoid planting in high traffic areas.

Indian hawthorne (Raphiolepis indica): Some cultivars of Indian hawthorne are small shrubs, making good substitutes for small azaleas in sunny spots. Pink or white flowers in spring. More tolerant of dry sites than azaleas. Very popular in the West, becoming very widely used here, too.

Gumpo azalea (Rhododendron eriocarpum): Small, compact, dense azalea. One of the Satsuki types. For fertile, moist, but well-drained sites. Partial shade best. Pink, white, or blush flowers in April or May.

Kurume azalea (Rhododendron obtusum): Hardy, mid-size azaleas, some over 4 ft. tall. Not for dry areas or poorly aerated areas. Our most common "dwarf" azaleas. Covered with masses of flowers in spring, ranging from white and soft pastels to vibrant reds and pinks. Normally bloom in March.

Satsuki azaleas (Rhododendron spp.): Group of April-May blooming azaleas. Not for dry, hot, or poorly aerated areas. Typically have strong horizontal growth habit and flowers larger than other "dwarf" azaleas.

Floribunda roses (Rosa floribunda): Though roses in general require high maintenance levels, some such as 'Eutin', 'Bonica', and 'Nearly Wild', require less. For full sun only. Perform best in fertile, moist, but well-drained soil. Bloom in cycles from April through November.

MEDIUM SHRUBS (4-8 FT.)

Abelia (Abelia grandiflora): White flowers all summer. Tough plant, tolerant of wide range of soil conditions. Good for hedges. Sun to part shade. 'Edward Goucher' not quite as tall and has pink flowers. Butterflies and bees love abelia.

Aucuba (Aucuba japonica): For shade only. Has green or variegated (depending on cultivar) evergreen, tropical-looking leaves. Tolerates wide range of soil conditions. Excellent plant as long as enough shade is provided.

Japanese barberry (Berberis thunbergi): Deciduous. Depending on cultivar, red leaves through part or all of growing season. Spines on stems. For sun to part shade. Tolerant of most soils.

Beautyberry (Callicarpa americana): Deciduous native shrub. Bears bright purple berries in fall, attractive to wildlife. White-berried cultivar also available. Prefers light shade and fertile, moist soil.

Sweetshrub (Calycanthus florida): Deciduous native shrub with fragrant, though not particularly showy, spring flowers. Sun to shade. Not highly tolerant of dry sites.

Sasanqua camellia (Camellia sasanqua): Some cultivars such as 'Shishi gashira' are relatively low-growing; others would be considered large shrubs. Glossy, dark-green foliage year-round. Flowers in white or shades of pinks and reds from fall to February. Excellent plant for partial shade or filtered sunlight; fertile, moist, but well-drained soils.

European fan palm (Chamaerops humilis): Very slow-growing to 12 ft. Beautiful, clumping palm for sun to part shade, wide range of soil types. Tolerant of cold to about 10 degrees F. if not for extended period.

Sago palm (Cycas revoluta): Palm-like, though not a true palm, very slowly growing to no more than 6 ft. Leaves killed by 10 degrees or below but plant will survive. Sun to shade, tolerant of wide range of sites. A good accent plant.

Fatsia (Fatsia japonica): Has large green, very tropical-like leaves. Needs shade or partial shade. Tolerant of all but very dry, hot sites.

Forsythia (Forsythia spp.): Deciduous shrub with brilliant yellow flowers in spring if enough cold received that winter. For sunny sites. Tolerates wide range of soil conditions except very dry ones.

Gardenia or cape jasmine (Gardenia jasminoides): Old Southern favorite, evergreen with very, very uniquely fragrant white summer flowers. Whiteflies are a major pest, with sooty mold resulting. Part shade to sun, well-drained, fertile, moist soils - good sites only.

Hydrangea (Hydrangea macrophylla): Deciduous shrub, producing pink or blue flower clusters in summer. Flower color depends on soil pH: acid soils produce blue flowers and basic or alkaline soils produce pink flowers. For shade or partial shade, moist, fertile, but well-drained soil.

Oakleaf hydrangea (Hydrangea quercifolia): Deciduous, native hydrangea producing white flower clusters in late spring. Red leaves in fall. For shade to partial shade, fertile, moist, well-drained soil.

Dwarf Burford holly (Ilex cornuta 'Burfordi Nana'): A versatile 6-10 ft. evergreen shrub with dark green glossy leaves. Only moderate berry production. Requires minimal pruning. For sun to moderate shade. Tolerant of wide range of soil conditions. Typically grows to 5-6 ft. Has large spiny evergreen leaves, clusters of large red berries. For sun to moderate shade. Tolerates wide range of soil conditions.

Gallberry or inkberry (Ilex glabra): A native evergreen with light green leaves. To 10 ft. tall. Has black berries during fall and winter. Sun to part shade. Moist, acid soils.

Blue Vase juniper (Juniperus chinesis 'Blue Vase'): 4-6 ft. tall evergreen with blue-green needle foliage. 4-6 ft. wide spread. For sun only, well-drained soils, tolerate dry sites. Give it plenty of room or it will look unnatural.

Pfitzer juniper (Juniperus chinensis 'Pfitzeriana'): Needle-like foliage evergreen with rapid growth to 6 ft. tall and 10-12 ft. spread. Too large for most foundation plantings. For sunny sites and wide ranges of soil conditions with exception of poorly drained or wet soils.

Texas sage (Leucophyllum frutescens): Silvery-gray, evergreen foliage. Lavender to pink flowers. For dry, sunny sites. Adds interesting foliage color to the landscape and is good for dry sites, but is not particularly long-lived.

Leatherleaf mahonia or Oregon grape holly (Mahonia bealei): Thick, spiny, evergreen leaves on canes; few branches. Leaves clustered at tips usually. Clusters of blue berries are especially attractive to mockingbirds. For shade to sun. Tolerant of all but wet, poorly drained soils.

Fortune's mahonia (Mahonia fortunei): Deep evergreen somewhat fern-like foliage. For part shade to shade. Prefers fertile, moist, well-drained soils -

good sites. Grows in an informal clump, with lanky stems sometimes falling over.

Nandina (Nandina domestica): Fast growing evergreen, producing red berries for winter. Cane-like growth. Very tough and versatile plant, tolerant of wide range of soil types. Sun to shade. Foliage takes on burgundy color in winter, especially in sun.

Indian hawthorne (Raphiolepis indica): Some cultivars are medium-sized shrubs, others are small. All are evergreen. Have either white or pink flowers. For sun to partial shade, well-drained soils.

Needle palm (Rhapidophyllum hystrix): Tough, versatile native shrubby palm. Very cold tolerant. Spines at base of plant cause temporarily painful wounds. Sun to shade. Tolerant of wide range of soil conditions.

Indica azaleas (Rhododendron indicum): The large azaleas of the Deep South. Many colors available. Prefer shade to partial shade, moist, fertile, well-drained soils. Not suited as a foundation planting for most buildings.

Saw palmetto (Serenoa repens): The dense native palmetto growth seen growing in pine woods across the South. Difficult to transplant and handle, though it is being used as an attractive addition in many new "natural" landscapes. Fairly tolerant of wide range of growing conditions.

Spirea (Spiraea spp.): Several species of deciduous, white spring-flowing shrubs. Graceful, informal style. Sun to partial shade. Fertile, moist but well-drained soils are best. Beautiful when used as an informal hedge or shrub border as on many old rural home sites.

Sandankwa viburnum (Viburnum suspensum): Dark green leaves with slightly roughened upper surface. Evergreen. Sun to shade, tolerant of wide range of soil conditions.

Weigelia (Weigelia florida): Deciduous plant with arching form. White, red, pink, or purple spring flowers. Not that attractive rest of year. Sun to part shade. Flowers poorly if not enough winter chilling received.

LARGE SHRUBS (8 FT. AND LARGER)

Bottlebrush buckeye (Aesculus parviflora): Deciduous native shrub for full sun or partial shade and fertile, moist but well-drained soils. Showy white flower clusters in early summer.

Red buckeye (Aesculus pavia): Deciduous native shrub or small tree for full sun to shade and fertile, moist but well-drained soils. Red flowers in spring.

Eastern baccharis (Baccharis halimifolia): Dull grayish green, evergreen leaves on 12 ft. plant. Native, salt-tolerant; tolerant of dry soils. White, feathery hairs on fruiting structures in fall are somewhat showy. For full sun. Not extremely attractive, but very tough. Not readily available in nurseries.

Bottlebrush (Callistemon rigidus): Red, bottle-brush-like flowers on evergreen shrub. For full sun, well-drained soils. Sensitive to hard freezes.

Camellia (Camellia japonica): Evergreen shrub for part shade to shade and fertile, moist, but well-drained soils. Flowers various shades and combinations of pinks, red, and whites from fall through late winter, exact time depending on cultivar. Beautiful dark green, glossy foliage year-round.

Sasanqua camellia (Camellia sasanqua): Fall and winter blooming evergreen. For shade to partial shade. Size depends on cultivar, but generally smaller than regular camellias. Some cultivars would be considered small to medium shrubs, particularly those with spreading forms. Need fertile, moist, but well-drained soil. Typically blooms earlier than *Camellia japonica.*

Silverthorn (Elaeagnus pungens): Extremely durable evergreen plant for wide range of soil conditions, sun to part shade. Needs plenty of room as it send up vigorous shoots from top, giving constant unkempt appearance if you try to maintain it as a clipped hedge. But makes good informal hedge. Fast grower.

Japanese euonymus (Euonymus japonica): Evergreen for sun to shade and wide range of soil types. Susceptibility to scale insects and powdery mildew limit its usefulness. Some cultivars are variegated.

Feijoa (Feijoa sellowiana): Gray-green evergreen foliage. For well-drained or even dry soils and sun or part shade. White, fragrant spring flowers with bright red stamens. Followed by small, edible fruit. Good hedge plant, though not overly showy.

Althea or Rose of Sharon (Hibiscus syriacus): Very common deciduous, cold-hardy hibiscus. Many flower variations of white, red, to almost blue. Prefers full sun. Tolerant of wide range of soil types.

Burford holly (Ilex cornuta 'Burfordii'): Rich, glossy evergreen leaves with red berries. Only one spine at tip of leaves. Rapid grower to 12-20 ft. For sun to shade. Best in fertile, moist, but well-drained soils.

Deciduous holly or possum haw (Ilex decidua): Deciduous holly with orange to scarlet fruits in fall persisting into winter for spectacular show once leaves drop. Attractive to birds. Partial shade to full sun and wet to dry soils.

Yaupon holly (Ilex vomitoria): Large native evergreen shrub or, more typically, small tree, for sun to shade, wet or dry sites. Female provides small red berries for birds.

Nellie R. Stevens holly (Ilex x 'Nellie R. Stevens'): Hybrid evergreen holly. Very durable and drought resistant. Tolerates wetter soils, too. Heavy red berry producer. Pyramidal growth habit.

Japanese anise (Illicium anisatum): Has light green, evergreen foliage with rootbeer fragrance when crushed. Unusual upright leaf orientation. Excellent hedge plant for part shade. Will tolerate shade or light sun. Tolerant of most soils except extremely dry or extremely wet. Very cold-hardy.

Hetzi juniper (Juniperus chinensis 'Hetzi'): Rapidly growing evergreen with needle-like foliage. To 8-10 ft. tall and even wider. For full sun and well-drained soils. Tolerant of dry sites. Attractive bluish color.

Torulosa or Hollywood juniper (Juniperus chinensis 'Torulosa'): Twisting, slender upright juniper to 12 ft. or so. For full sun and well-drained soils. Tolerant of dry sites. Dramatic effect; don't overuse within a single landscape.

Florida leucothoe (Leucothoe populifolia): Native evergreen with somewhat irregular growth habit. Needs pruning to stay fairly full. For shade to part shade only and fertile, moist, but well-drained soils.

Japanese or waxleaf ligustrum (Ligustrum japonicum): Very tough, versatile, and rapidly growing shrub with waxy, green evergreen leaves. For sun to shade and wide range of sites and soil conditions. Fragrant white spring flowers may be troublesome to people with allergies.

Glossy ligustrum (Ligustrum lucidum): A larger ligustrum, very adaptable to a wide range of sites, sun or shade. Tends to be a heavy seeder and can become a problem sprouting up around the landscape. Leaves not as glossy as *L. japonicum*. Rapid grower. Attracts whiteflies, but they don't seem to injure it.

Variegated Chinese ligustrum (Ligustrum sinense 'Variegata'): Small white to yellowish variegated leaves on rapidly growing plant to about 12 ft. tall. Is very tolerant of pruning; in fact, will need some pruning to look its best. Whiteflies and white peach scale can be problems. For sun to shade, though a little more open and spindly in shade. Fairly tolerant of various soil types.

Banana shrub (Michelia fuscata): Evergreen with small yellow spring flowers having a strong banana-like scent that can be smelled from quite a distance. For sun to part shade. Needs fertile, moist, but well-drained soil. A southern classic.

Wax myrtle (Myrica cerifera): One of the most versatile and durable of evergreen shrubs or small trees. For wet or dry sites, sun or shade. Prune as tree, large shrub, or hedge. Virtually carefree. Suckers from the base. Female plants provide gray berries for birds.

Oleander (Nerium oleander): Flowering, fast-growing evergreen shrub. Leaves may brown during hard freezes. Flowers of pink, red, white, or yellow borne in summer. For full sun. Tolerant of variety of soil types. Very salt tolerant. All parts poisonous if eaten.

Fortunes osmanthus (Osmanthus fortunei): Evergreen with spiny leaves. Flowers are not noteworthy. For full sun or partial shade and fertile, moist, but well-drained soils.

Tea olive (Osmanthus fragrans): Evergreen with small, but very fragrant white flowers in fall and spring. For full sun or partial shade and fertile, moist, but well-drained soils. Very popular because of the long periods of fragrant flowers. A Southern favorite.

Fraser photinia (Photinia x 'Fraseri'): Evergreen shrub with red foliage. For sun to part shade. Not for poorly drained or exceptionally dry soils. Leaf spot disease can be somewhat of a problem.

Redtop or redtip photinia (Photinia glabra): Evergreen shrub. New foliage is red. For sun to part shade. Not for poorly drained or exceptionally dry soils. Leaf spot disease has become such a serious problem, especially on tightly clipped hedges, as to limit this plant's usefulness.

Chinese photinia (Photinia serrulata): A larger photinia with large glossy leaves. New leaves have red tint. Showy white flowers in spring, but flowers have an unpleasant odor. For fertile, moist, but well-drained sites. This plant is best reserved for very large landscapes.

Pittosporum (Pittosporum tobira): Green or variegated forms, both having evergreen foliage. Variegated form not as large. For sun to shade and dry or moderately wet soils. Very fragrant spring flowers. Good, versatile plants.

Yew podocarpus (Podocarpus macrophyllus): Evergreen shrub with very dark and slender foliage and columnar form. Easily shaped and controlled; versatile for a variety of uses. For sun to shade. Not for poorly drained soil. A favorite of aphids, but can tolerate high populations without damage.

Nagi podocarpus (Podocarpus nagi): A broader-leafed podocarpus, making a striking accent plant. For sun or shade. Not for poorly drained soils.

Cherry laurel (Prunus caroliniana): Vigorous, adaptable large native evergreen shrub or small tree. Commonly sprouts from seed spread by birds. Sun to part shade and moist, fertile, but well-drained soils.

Firethorn (Pyracantha coccinea): Evergreen noted for orange berries from fall through winter. Has thorns that can be quite painful. Somewhat rangy grower. Needs plenty of room to grow and cascade as natural growth habit. Very attractive where it has room to grow without over-pruning. For sun and well-drained soils. Mockingbirds love the berries.

Formosan firethorn (Pyracantha koidzumii): Pyracantha with red berries. Larger grower.

Florida azalea (Rhododendron austrinum): Deciduous native azalea with fragrant, golden yellow flowers in late March or early April. Needs a good, moist, but well-drained acid soil and a partially shaded site shielded from harsh heat.

Piedmont azalea (Rhododendron canescens): Another common native, deciduous azalea. Depending on the particular plant, fragrant flowers range from pure white to deep pink. Blooms in late March or early April. Needs fertile, acidic, moist, but well-drained soil and a partially shaded site. Suckers prolifically.

Shining or winged sumac (Rhus copallina): A native deciduous plant, making a good small tree or large shrub. Brilliant red leaves in fall. Fruit, ripening in fall, attractive to birds. Tolerant of dry sites. For sun to partial shade. Has wings along stem of the leaves.

Is not the same plant as poison sumac. Suckers prolifically.

Cleyera (Ternstroemia japonica): Not to be confused with *Cleyera japonica*, Japanese cleyera, which requires shade. Ternstroemia is a versatile evergreen for sun or shade and fertile, moist, but well-drained soils. Rich, dark, glossy green foliage with colorful wine-red new growth. Easily shaped.

Oriental arborvitae (Thuja orientalis): Cheap, overused, needle evergreen, very susceptible to juniper blight, bagworms, and spider mites. For sun to part shade. Tolerant of all but extremely wet, poorly drained soils.

Sweet viburnum (Viburnum odoratissimum): Evergreen shrub, tolerating most soils. For partial shade to sun, preferring partial shade. Very good hedge plant. Gets whiteflies but they don't seem to harm the plant. Clusters of fragrant, white flowers in the spring if the plant isn't pruned too severely. *V. odoratissimum* is cold-hardy to the mid-teens.

Sandanqua viburnum (Viburnum suspensum): Not as fast or large a grower as *V. odoratissimum*. Leaves have wrinkled appearance on surface.

SHRUBS FOR DRY, SUNNY SITES—TOLERANT OF DROUGHT

Abelia (*Abelia grandiflora*)
Eastern baccharis (*Baccharis halimifolia*)
Barberry (*Berberis spp.*)
Beautyberry (*Callicarpa americana*)
Bottlebrush (*Callistemon rigidus*)
Sago palm (*Cycas revoluta*)
Elaeagnus (*Elaeagnus pungens*)
Feijoa (*Feijoa sellowiana*)
Gallberry (*Ilex glabra*)
Yaupon (*Ilex vomitoria*)
Junipers (*Juniperus spp.*)
Texas sage (*Leucophyllum frutescens*)
Ligustrums (*Ligustrum spp.*)
Wax myrtle (*Myrica cerifera*)
Oleander (*Nerium oleander*)
Redtop (*Photinia glabra*)
Photinia (*Photinia spp.*)
Pittosporum (*Pittosporum tobira*)
Yew podocarpus (*Podocarpus macrophyllus*)
Cherry laurel (*Prunus caroliniana*)
Pyracantha (*Pyracantha spp.*)
Indian hawthorne (*Raphiolepis spp.*)

Needle palm (*Rhapidophyllum hystrix*)
Sumac (*Rhus spp.*)
Saw palmetto (*Serenoa repens*)
Spiraea (*Spiraea spp.*)
Windmill palm (*Trachycarpus fortunei*)

SHRUBS FOR SHADED AREAS

Aucuba (*Aucuba japonica*)
Fatsia (*Fatsia japonica*)
Hydrangea (*Hydrangea macrophylla*)
Oakleaf hydrangea (*Hydrangea quercifolia*)
Deciduous holly or possumhaw (*Ilex decidua*)
Florida leucothoe (*Leucothoe populifolia*)
Mahonia (*Mahonia spp.*)
Wax myrtle (*Myrica cerifera*)
Nandina (*Nandina domestica*)
Pittosporum (*Pittosporum tobira*)
Needle palm (*Rhapidophyllum hystrix*)
Azaleas (*Rhododendron spp.*)
Cleyera (*Ternstroemia japonica*)
Windmill palm (*Trachycarpus fortunei*)
Viburnum (*Viburnum spp.*)

SHRUBS FOR PARTIALLY SHADED AREAS

Abelia (*Abelia grandiflora*)
Boxwood (*Buxus spp.*)
Camellia (*Camellia spp.*)
European fan palm (*Chamaerops humilis*)
Silverthorn (*Elaeagnus pungens*)
Fatsia (*Fatsia japonica*)
Feijoa (*Feijoa sellowiana*)
Gardenia (*Gardenia spp.*)
Hydrangea (*Hydrangea macrophylla*)
Oakleaf hydrangea (*Hydrangea quercifolia*)
Hollies (*Ilex spp.*)
Japanese anise (*Illicium anisatum*)
Florida leucothoe (*Leucothoe populifolia*)
Ligustrum (*Ligustrum spp.*)
Mahonia (*Mahonia spp.*)
Wax myrtle (*Myrica cerifera*)
Nandina (*Nandina domestica*)
Pittosporum (*Pittosporum tobira*)
Cherry laurel (*Prunus caroliniana*)
Indian hawthorne (*Raphiolepis indica*)
Needle palm (*Rhapidophyllum hystrix*)
Azaleas (*Rhododendron spp.*)
Cleyera (*Ternstroemia japonica*)
Windmill palm (*Trachycarpus fortunei*)

Viburnum (*Viburnum spp.*)

SHRUBS FOR WET SITES, POORLY DRAINED AREAS

Sweetshrub (*Calycanthus floridus*)
Sweet pepperbush (*Clethra alnifolia*)
Silverthorn (*Elaeagnus pungens*)
Euonymus (*Euonymus japonica*)
Oakleaf hydrangea (*Hydrangea quercifolia*)
Chinese hollies (*Ilex cornuta*)
Deciduous holly (*Ilex decidua*)
Inkberry or gallberry (*Ilex glabra*)
American holly (*Ilex opaca*)
Florida leucothoe (*Leucothoe populifolia*)
Ligustrum (*Ligustrum spp.*)
Wax myrtle (*Myrica cerifera*)
Oleander (*Nerium oleander*)
Tea olive (*Osmanthus fragrans*)
Cherry laurel (*Prunus caroliniana*)
Needle palm (*Rhapidophyllum hystrix*)
Windmill palm (*Trachycarpus fortunei*)

SALT-TOLERANT SHRUBS

Eastern baccharis (*Baccharis halimifolia*)
Bottlebrush (*Callistemon spp.*)
Sago palm (*Cycas revoluta*)
Silverthorn (*Elaeagnus pungens*)
Euonymus (*Euonymus japonica*)
Fatsia (*Fatsia japonica*)
Feijoa (*Feijoa sellowiana*)
Althea (*Hibiscus syriacus*)
Burford holly (*Ilex cornuta 'Burfordii'*)
Inkberry (*Ilex glabra*)
Yaupon holly (*Ilex vomitoria*)
Dwarf yaupon holly (*Ilex vomitoria 'Nana'*)
Chinese juniper (*Juniperus chinensis*)
Texas sage (*Leucophyllum frutescens*)
Ligustrum (*Ligustrum spp.*)
Leatherleaf mahonia (*Mahonia bealei*)
Wax myrtle (*Myrica cerifera*)
Oleander (*Nerium oleander*)
Pittosporum (*Pittosporum tobira*)
Broadleaf podocarpus (*Podocarpus nagi*)
Pyracantha (*Pyracantha spp.*)
Indian hawthorne (*Raphiolepis indica*)
Rose (*Rosa spp.*)
Sweet viburnum (*Viburnum odoratissimum*)

Sandankwa viburnum (*Viburnum suspensum*)

SHRUBS FOR HEDGES

Abelia
Anise
Indica azaleas
Boxwoods
Camellias
Sasanqua camellias
Cherry laurel
Cleyera
Feijoa
Hollies (esp. 'Burford' and 'Dwarf Burford')
Chinese junipers ('Hetzi' and 'Pfitzer')
Ligustrums
Oleander
Photinia
Pittosporum
Podocarpus
Silverthorn (*Elaeagnus*)
Spirea
Viburnums
Wax myrtle

SHRUBS, VINES, AND SMALL TREES FOR FRAGRANCE

Sweet autumn clematis (*Clematis dioscorifolia*)
Sweet pepperbush (*Clethra alnifolia*)
Dogwood (*Cornus florida*)
Loquat (*Eriobotrya japonica*)
Gardenia (*Gardenia jasminoides*)
Carolina jessamine (*Gelsemium sempervirens*)
Banana shrub (*Michelia fuscata*)
Tea olive (*Osmanthus fragrans*)
Pittosporum (*Pittosporum tobira*)
Florida azalea (*Rhododendron canescens*)
Piedmont azalea (*Rhododendron canescens*)
Roses (*Rosa spp.*)

S hrub plantings are also useful in providing habitats and food for birds and other wildlife. See chapter 12 for more details on plantings for birds.

Confederate jasmine (*Trachelospermum jasminoides*)
Sweet viburnum (*Viburnum odoratissimum*)

PLANTING SHRUBS: SOME ADVICE

There's an adage that advises, "Don't plant a $10 shrub in a 50-cent hole." You would be wise to heed that advice.

The hole in which you plant a shrub should be at least twice as wide as the root ball of the shrub. Three times wide, or even wider, would be better. Don't worry about digging a deep hole. The plant only needs to be planted as deep as it was in the container or even a tiny bit higher. Never plant too deeply.

Before putting the soil back into the hole around the plant, thoroughly break up all clumps. Then gradually fill back in around the shrub's root ball, gently firming the soil as you go. Mulch the plant when you finish. Fertilize with a slow-release 16-4-8 or similar fertilizer. Water by hand, letting the water slowly soak into the soil.

The exact time it will take for the plant's roots to become established in the surrounding soil will vary with type of plant and environmental conditions. But, for the first year after planting, realize that the plant will still be relying largely on the roots in the original root ball. This limited root ball will be very susceptible to drying during periods of inadequate rainfall. So, it is important that you apply water whenever rainfall isn't adequate.

It is not longer recommended that soil amendments, such as peat, be mixed with the soil in individual planting holes. University research has shown no advantage to individually amending planting holes. Yet, there can be disadvantages in that water can stand in such amended holes, rotting roots. If you wish to use soil amendments, such as peat or compost, amend the entire planting bed, tilling the amendments in with the existing soil.

Before planting in poorly drained soils, please read Chapter 3 about planting in sites with poorly drained soils.

DETERMINING SPACING BETWEEN SHRUBS

It's often difficult to know how far apart to space shrubs in a planting. But those tiny one-gallon plants can often become quite large with time. And, unless you know the ultimate size of the plants, you may

COLORFUL SHRUBS

Shrub	What's Colorful	Time of Year
Abelia	White flowers	summer
Ardisia	red berries	winter
Aucuba	leaves	year-round
Azaleas	various flower colors	spring
Banana shrub	yellow flowers	spring
Barberry	leaves	year-round, winter
Beautyberry	purple fruit	fall
Bottlebrush	red flowers	late spring
Camellia	various flower colors	winter
Cherry laurel	white	spring
Chinese hollies	red berries	winter
Feijoa	white flowers, red stamens	spring
Forsythia	yellow flowers	spring
Gardenia	white flowers	spring
Hydrangea	blue, pink flowers	late spring
Indian hawthorne	white-pink flowers	spring
Leatherleaf mahonia	grape-like berries	summer
Ligustrum	white flowers	spring
Loropetalum	white or pink flowers	spring
Nandina	red berries	winter
Native azaleas	various flowers	spring
Oakleaf hydrangea	white flowers	late spring, summer
Oleander	red, pink, cream, white flowers	late spring, summer
Pyracantha	orange berries	fall-winter
Redtop photinia	red young foliage	year-round
Sasanqua camellias	various flower colors	fall-winter
Spiraea	white flowers	spring
Sweet viburnum	white flowers	spring
Tea olive	white	fall, winter, spring
Texas sage	lavender flowers	summer
Weigelia	pink, red, white flowers	spring
Yaupon holly	red berries	winter

overplant and reduce the effective life of the planting by creating overcrowded growing conditions.

Below are listed some common types of shrubs and recommended planting spacings. You can use these spacings as recommendations for other similar shrubs, too.

Most spreading junipers: Space 3 ft. from walls, fences, or buildings. Space 3-4 ft. between centers of plants for ground cover uses. Space 3 ½ ft. from walks or drives.

Dwarf Japanese Garden Junipers: Space 3 ft. from walls, fences, or buildings. Space 2-2 ½ ft. from walks or drives. Space 3 ½-4 ½ ft. between centers for a mass effect.

Dwarf Azaleas and other slow-growing small shrubs: Space 3 ft. from walls, fences, buildings, walks, or drives. Space 3 ft. between centers of plants.

Dwarf yaupons, rotunda hollies, boxwoods,

nandina, mahonia, and other small to medium-size shrubs: Space 3 ft. from walls, fences, or buildings. Space 2 ft. from walks or drives. Space 3-4 ft. between centers for a mass planting effect. Space 5-6 ft. between centers if the appearance of individual plants is wanted.

Podocarpus, upright sasanqua cultivars, and other strongly upright-growing shrubs: Space 3 ft. from walls, fences, or buildings. Space 3 ½-4 ft. between centers for groupings, 2-3 ft. for hedges, and 4 ½-5 ft. where the appearance of individual specimens is wanted.

Cleyera, Sandankwa viburnum, and other fairly compact but large shrubs: Space 4-5 ft. from walls, fences, or buildings. Space 4 ft. between centers for clipped hedges, 4-5 ft. between centers in groupings, and 5-6 ft. between centers for the appearance of individual specimens.

Spirea, Indica azaleas, forsythia, and dwarf Burford hollies (medium to large, somewhat spreading shrubs): Space 3 ½ ft. from walls, fences, or buildings. Space 4-5 ft. between centers for a mass planting and 6-8 ft. for the appearance of individual specimens.

Pittosporum, Burford holly, camellia, and sasanqua (large, but not the largest of shrubs): Space 5-6 ft. from walls, fences, or buildings. Space 6-8 ft. between centers for a grouping effect; space 4-6 ft. for a clipped hedge.

Pyracantha, elaeagnus, and other large, unruly shrubs: Space 5 ½-6 ft. from walls, fences, or buildings. Space 8-10 ft. between centers in mass plantings. Space 10-12 ft. between centers for individual specimen effect.

Common tea olive, camellia, Frazier's photinia, and other large shrubs/small trees: Space 8-12 ft. between centers in naturalized groupings. Space 7-8 ft. between centers for screening. Space 5-6 ft. between centers for a clipped hedge - probably not a good use for most plants in this group - they're just too naturally large to be maintained as a clipped hedge.

FERTILIZING SHRUBS

To fertilize shrubs and small trees, use about two teaspoons of a 16-4-8 or similar fertilizer (with 8% water-insoluble nitrogen) per foot of plant height. Small shrubs, less than a foot tall, should receive no more than one level teaspoon.

Another way to figure fertilizer rates is on the basis of applying one pound of actual nitrogen per 1,000 sq. ft.. For example, apply 6 pounds of 16-4-8 per 1,000 sq. ft. Or, apply 8 lbs. of 12-4-8, 7 lbs. of 13-6-6, etc. Just divide the first fertilizer analysis number into 100 to determine the correct rate per 1,000 sq. ft.

There is no need to pull the mulch back before fertilizing. When fertilizing shrubs and trees, just spread the fertilizer on the ground beneath the branch spread and slightly beyond. Water to wash it down through the mulch or grass.

Don't fertilize any more than necessary. All plants need nutrients. But, if you manage your landscape correctly, by the time your trees and shrubs are older, a nutrient recycling system should be in place. It's the new, young trees and shrubs in your landscape that most need the fertilizer to grow.

When you're trying to encourage very young trees and shrubs to grow, you can fertilize up to four times a growing season (in March, May, July, and September). But, moderate growth can be obtained with applications only in March and July.

Mature shrubs can often get by with only the March application. In fact, if you keep a 2-inch thick layer of pine straw or leaf mulch around the plants, mature shrubs may need no yearly fertilization. The nutrients released from the mulch breakdown is sometimes enough. Let the appearance and the vigor of the shrubs guide you in determining the necessity and frequency of fertilization. You'll find that plants growing in sandy soils will require fertilization more often than those growing in heavier soils.

WATERING SHRUBS

Once shrubs become well established, you will find that you rarely need to water them. Only during very dry weather will rainfall not provide for their needs - if you have selected the proper shrubs for the site and have kept them mulched.

Some shrubs, such as azaleas or hydrangeas, will readily tell you with drooping leaves when they need water. Water stress may be more difficult to detect in shrubs with stiffer leaves. To check moisture needs of such shrubs during periods of longer-than-normal dry weather, develop the habit of occasionally monitoring the soil moisture level by digging in the soil with a garden trowel or with your hand. Be sure to check 4 inches or so down rather than just scratch the soil surface. If the soil is cool and moist enough to stick together when squeezed, there's probably adequate moisture.

When you do have to water, water deeply, applying an inch of water if you can do so without it running off. Deep watering encourages deep rooting. And, deep rooting results in stronger, more drought tolerant plants. Frequent, shallow watering does just the opposite.

Of course, when you have just planted shrubs, and their roots are still restricted to the container root ball (they haven't ventured out, taking anchor in the surrounding soil yet), you will need to water more frequently. You may need to water as often as daily if it's summer and you've planted one-gallon plants in sandy soil. The key lies in not letting the roots dry out but not keeping them saturated either. You will simply have to feel the soil in the root zone to determine when to water. There is no hard and fast rule because there are too many variables such as soil type, time of year, size of plant, type of plant, etc.

WEED CONTROL AROUND SHRUBS

Most of your shrubs should be in groups with other shrubs. Minimize your plantings of individual shrubs out in the lawn and you'll greatly reduce the maintenance required. It's much easier to maintain a bed of shrubs than it is to maintain scattered shrubs here and there.

Maintain a mulch of pine straw, bark, or other organic material on the ground beneath the shrubs. If you have a hedge or other row of shrubs, don't simply mulch in little rings around each plant so that you still have to mow between plants. Rather, mulch the entire bed.

A generous 2-inch layer of mulch is your best method of weed control around shrubs. The mulch will also prevent the soil from packing and stunting the shrubs' growth. In addition, the mulch will moderate soil temperatures, conserve moisture, provide nutrients, and be attractive and neat.

Weeds that pop up through the mulch layer can be either hand pulled or spot treated with a herbicide containing glyphosate (such as Roundup®). Keep any herbicide mist whatsoever, though, off the foliage of the shrubs. Never spray when there is any wind.

Weeds will be their worst the first 2-3 years after planting a new area. If you keep the area mulched, though, the weed problem will reduce drastically after several years.

The selection of selective herbicides (those that can be applied over the general area, killing the weed and not the desired plants) is very limited for use around shrubs. There are a couple that can be applied over the top of certain shrubs to kill existing weeds. But, these herbicides aren't approved for use on all types of shrubs. Nor are they effective on all weeds. Consequently, they are rarely used in landscape situations.

There are a few pre-emergent herbicides (to be applied after weeds are hand pulled or spot-treated and before new ones emerge) available from garden centers. Again, these herbicides aren't approved for use on all shrubs; nor are they effective on all weeds. Read the label carefully before using any such herbicide. Apply the herbicide exactly as the label specifies.

> The bottom line is that there is no selective herbicide that will totally take the place of a good mulch used with occasional hand-pulling or spot-treating.

7
Lawns

Avoiding the Headaches

HOW LARGE SHOULD YOUR LAWN BE?

Just about everyone has a lawn, probably a larger one than is necessary. Lawns have many functional purposes. For example, lawns are great places for kids of all ages to play. And, lawns can be very attractive in themselves.

But lawns require more work than any other part of your landscape. They must be fertilized, watered at times, and mowed regularly. At times they may even have to be de-thatched, aerated, or sprayed for pests. Hundreds of millions of dollars, maybe even billions, are spent each year on lawn care in the United States.

What other plant do you fertilize, water, and baby along only to remove its new growth every week? Sounds ridiculous when you think about it, doesn't it?

Lawns present another problem here in the South. The lawn grasses grown here will not tolerate shade very well. St. Augustine grass, our most shade-tolerant of southern lawn grasses, still needs a fair bit of sun to grow well. Yet most homeowners want a lawn with trees in it. That just will not work well.

For these reasons, I propose that many people have too much lawn. Personally, I've decreased the lawn area in my yard each time I move to a new home. Hopefully, my next home will have an even smaller lawn. My ideal landscape would consist of mostly trees, shrubs, ground covers, and flower beds. I would still have a small lawn; I truly enjoy the sight of a green carpet in the landscape. But I view a lawn as just one small part of a landscape. Too many people view it as the main part. I feel that a lawn that can be mowed in half an hour or less will satisfy most families' needs for a green carpet.

WHAT'S THE BEST KIND OF LAWN GRASS?

There is no one perfect type of southern lawn grass. All the grasses have their problems and their strong points.

Centipede is a common grass in many areas, readily available as sod or seed. It is not salt tolerant and so shouldn't be planted where it will receive salt spray. it is only fairly tolerant of shade. It doesn't tolerate heavy foot traffic or other wear well. But, it doesn't require high levels of fertilizer. And, it only has to be mowed every 7-14 days. Nematodes can sometimes be a serious problem on centipede.

St. Augustine is the grass most commonly planted along the coast because it is salt tolerant. Many people don't like its coarse texture. But, it tolerates wear fairly well and doesn't have excessively high maintenance requirements. Thatch, though, is more of a problem than with centipede. St. Augustine grass

> **L**awns present another problem here in the South. The lawn grasses grown here will not tolerate shade very well.

cannot be started from seed. Nematodes are occasionally a problem for St. Augustine grass.

Most kinds of St. Augustine grass are more tolerant of shade than are other southern grasses. 'Floratam', the chinch bug resistant cultivar of St. Augustine grass, though, is not shade tolerant. Nor is it very cold hardy. It is best used in central and south Florida. Other cultivars of St. Augustine grass are better suited for most of the lower South.

Zoysia grass has received a lot of promotion in ads as the "miracle grass." However, despite the promotions, it is not the perfect grass either. It is slow to spread and slow to recover from damage. And, because it grows so thickly, thatch can be a problem. Zoysia should be mowed with a reel mower rather than a rotary mower to prevent scalping. Zoysia cannot be started from seed.

On the other hand, zoysia grass has excellent drought tolerance and wear tolerance. It is also salt tolerant. Zoysia is well-liked because of its fine texture and soft feel. It has fair shade tolerance.

Bahia grass is excellent in terms of being tough as nails. It is extremely drought tolerant, has good wear tolerance, and doesn't require much fertilizer. But, bahia grass produces a tall Y-shaped seed head quickly during the growing season that requires it to be mowed every 5-7 days during the growing season for optimal appearance. Bahia grass can be seeded. It has very poor shade tolerance and salt tolerance. 'Argentine' bahia is preferred over 'Pensacola' bahia for lawns because seed heads are not as numerous.

Hybrid bermuda grasses will grow well in the South, but they are not used as often because of their high maintenance requirements. They must be fertilized and mowed more often than the other warm-season lawn grasses. And, they look much better if mowed with a reel-type mower. Despite these high maintenance consideration, hybrid bermuda grasses have a high wear tolerance and quick recovery rate from damage. Consequently, they're usually the grasses of choice for athletic fields and golf courses.

Common bermuda grass, often a weed in flower or shrub beds or the vegetable garden, is not often used as a lawn grass. It is the only bermuda grass that can be started from seed, but it lacks the fine appearance of the hybrid bermudas. The required maintenance level for an attractive lawn is more or less the same as for the hybrid bermudas. Common bermuda is usually reserved for uses such as roadsides, etc., where toughness and rate of growth is more important than appearance.

Carpet grass is only suitable as a lawn grass in areas which stay constantly very wet. It is extremely intolerant of dry conditions and should not be used on most sites.

THE FOLLOWING LAWN CARE CAN PREVENT MANY PROBLEMS

Chances are that if you have a lawn you'll have problems with it from time to time. Most problems are related to care of the lawn. So, let's talk about lawn care and about potential problems.

THE NUMBER ONE LAWN PROBLEM: POOR SOIL CONDITIONS

Many lawn problems can be traced to the fact that the soil is too hard to allow good root growth. It pays to properly prepare the soil before planting your lawn. Thoroughly rototill the entire area before planting. Then rake the area to smooth it. Water the soil to settle it. If the site has been scraped of its topsoil, you may have to add topsoil or other soil amendments during the rototilling stage. Avoid the common mistake of planting sod on compacted soil that is too hard to invite good growth. It is impossible to totally correct the situation later.

Short of starting over and properly tilling the area, maybe adding some soil amendments, about all you can do to an existing lawn is call in a lawn service to aerate the area with a heavy-duty core type aerating machine. This will cultivate the soil by pulling plugs out, allowing better penetration of air, water, and fertilizer.

Don't forget that any type of frequent traffic, foot, automobile, even dog traffic, can compact the soil and cause poor grass growth of an exis-ting lawn.

ADEQUATE SUNLIGHT

Many lawn problems can be traced to the fact that the soil is too hard to allow good root growth.

Too often, we try to grow grass in areas of inadequate sunlight. St. Augustine is our most shade-tolerant lawn grass, but even St. Augustine grass will tolerate only so much shade. If you insist on growing grass in a shaded area, I suggest plugging in St. Augustine (avoid the 'Floratam' cultivar if the shade is heavy, as 'Floratam' is the least shade-tolerant St. Augustine). If your test plugs don't take off and grow within a month or so, you probably just have too much shade, provided you give the grass water, good soil, and other things it needs to grow. If it does grow well, then convert the area over from centipede or other present grass to St. Augustine grass.

WATERING

Lawn grasses usually require supplemental watering at times to grow well, and most people know that. Unfortunately, though, few people really water correctly and that contributes to many of our lawn problems.

Water only when needed. Only when the grass turns that wilted gray-green color should you water. But then, water deeply, applying ½ to ¾ inch of water so that the entire root zone will be wet. So often we don't water long enough, and a shallow grass root system is the result.

The only way to tell how long you should water is to place cups or rain gauges out in the sprinkler pattern to catch water for 15 minutes. Measure the amount of water in each cup and then take the average amount of water in the cups. Multiply that average amount by 4 to obtain the hourly watering rate. Suppose it is ¼ inch. Then you know you'll need to run the water 3 hours in that spot to apply ¾ inch of water, the desired amount.

> *Only when the grass turns that wilted gray-green color should you water. But then, water deeply, applying ½ to ¾ inch of water so that the entire root zone will be wet. So often we don't water long enough, and a shallow grass root system is the result.*

In summary, make sure you're watering long enough. But only water when it is really needed. Watering too shallowly and too frequently will lead to a multitude of problems. For instance, diseases are stimulated by a moist environment. Excess water also leads to excess growth which, in turn, leads to thatch problems.

Many of you have underground sprinkler systems complete with time-clocks. Turn the time-clock off for the most part. Rather, just set the clock to turn on the system on those occasional early morning hours it is needed. If you go on a vacation, set the time-clock to run the system every five days or so. And, by all means, take the time to measure the output from each zone of the system so you'll know how long each zone needs to run.

MOWING

Again, everyone thinks they know how to mow. But, so often, we mow the grass too low and weaken it. Think about it. You do everything you can to grow good grass. Then when it grows up you scalp it down. How devastating to the grass!

Measure the height of your mower blade from a flat surface such as the driveway. It should be a minimum of 1 ½ inches high for mowing centipede and 3 inches minimum for mowing St. Augustine grass. Mow Bahia grass at 3-4 inches and Zoysia at 1-2 inches. Bermuda grass should be mowed at ½-1 inch and mowed with a reel mower (not a rotary mower). Mow on the higher end of these ranges when the grass is stressed by shade or other factors.

> *Don't bag the clippings when you mow. They do not contribute to thatch. Over-fertilizing and overwatering do more to cause thatch, an accumulation of old grass runners, not clippings. Clippings, on the other hand, are good for the grass because they contain nutrients. You need to recycle them.*

Don't bag the clippings when you mow. They do not contribute to thatch. Over-fertilizing and over-watering do more to cause thatch, an accumulation of old grass runners, not clippings. Clippings, on the other hand, are good for the grass because they contain nutrients. You need to recycle them back into the lawn. Also, you'll save much time if you don't bag, even if you have to mow the lawn a little more often. Actually, you probably won't have to mow more often. Try it; I think you'll like it.

One last note on mowing: Sharpen that mower blade every month. Not only will it make mowing easier, but it will make your grass look better and be healthier. Shredded blades are an invitation for disease problems and give the entire lawn a brownish cast.

FERTILIZING

Your grass needs nutrients. But too rich of a supply leads to pest problems taking advantage of the lush growth. And, it means you'll have more of a mowing problem.

Use a fertilizer with slow-release nitrogen to avoid that fast rush of nitrogen availability and lush growth. Use 16-4-8, 16-0-8, or a similar ratio, such as 32-0-16 or 12-4-8. All are close to 4-1-2, 4-0-2, or 3-1-2 ratios. Select one with half of the nitrogen listed on the label as water-insoluble. For example, in a 16-4-8 fertilizer, that would be 8% water-insoluble nitrogen. Also, select a fertilizer with at least 2% iron.

Avoid fertilizers such as 29-3-3, 23-3-3, etc. They are too high in nitrogen in relation to the phosphorous and potassium.

You'll pay more for a good fertilizer with water-insoluble nitrogen. But it will help you prevent problems in the long run.

When to fertilize: DO NOT fertilize in the spring until three weeks after the grass greens up and not before mid-March when danger of frost is usually past. Otherwise, yellowing may result. Centipede grass can often get by on one fertilization, and even occasionally none if you're not bagging clippings and if your soil is not overly sandy. If you have a sandy soil, or if your grass is growing poorly, you may need to come back with a second application in August.

St. Augustine grass might also get by on one spring application, but it is probably more common to apply a second in August. Bermuda grass and zoysia grass, on the other hand, will require fertilizer applications 2-3 times over the growing season.

How much fertilizer? One pound of actual nitrogen per 1,000 sq. ft. per application. That means 6-7 lbs. of 16-4-8, 8 lbs. of 12-4-8, etc. Divide the percentage of nitrogen (the first number) into 100 to obtain the number of pounds of fertilizer you'll need.

You'll just have to calibrate your spreader by putting in a known weight of fertilizer, apply-ing over a given area, and then re-weighing the spreader contents to determine amount applied over the given area. Adjust the spreader opening up or down accordingly. A broadcast spreader usually applies with less streaking than does a drip-type spreader. Don't use a broadcast spreader with weed-and-feed fertilizers, though.

What about "winterizer" fertilizers advertised in the fall? There is some truth to the claim that increased potassium (the third number in the fertilizer ration, eg., 14 in 10-5-14) increases cold hardiness of lawn grasses. More accurately, it is an increased potassium to nitrogen ratio that gives the grass cold hardiness. But, many so-called winterizers on the market are too high in nitrogen. Nitrogen should not be applied at a rate greater than ½ lb. of actual nitrogen per 1000 square feet after mid-September. If you apply a 10-5-14 winterizer, a common commercial analysis, at the rate of 0.5 lbs. of nitrogen per 1000 square feet, only 0.7 lbs. of potassium would be applied. A good winterizer should be lower in nitrogen. A 5-5-14, 5-2-14, or 5-0-14 would be better. You shouldn't even use such analyses as this later than mid-October, though.

There's probably no need to apply a winterizer at all if you applied a fertilizer such as 16-4-8 as late as August. Rather than applying the late summer fertilization of 16-4-8, you may prefer to use the 5-2-14 in September instead. Apply one or the other, but both are probably not needed.

> **U**se 16-4-8, 16-0-8, or a similar ratio, such as 32-0-16 or 12-4-8. All are close to 4-1-2, 4-0-2, or 3-1-2 ratios. Select one with half of the nitrogen listed on the bag as water-insoluble.

POSSIBLE FERTILIZER PROGRAMS FOR YOUR LAWN

Centipede: In late March to April, fertilize with a complete fertilizer such as 16-4-8, 16-0-8, 32-0-16 or similar fertilizer containing iron. In August, make another application of this fertilizer. Skip the August application if your lawn is growing vigorously and looks healthy already. Or wait until September and use 5-2-14 or similar winterizer.

St. Augustine grass: In late March to April, apply

a complete fertilizer such as 16-4-8, 16-0-8, or 32-0-16 with iron. In September, apply the same fertilizer again or use 5-2-14 or similar winterizer.

Bahia grass: In late March to April, apply a complete fertilizer such as 16-4-8, 16-0-8, 32-0-16, etc. containing iron. In September, apply the same fertilizer again unless your lawn is growing vigorously and looks healthy. You could substitute a 5-2-14 or similar winterizer for the September application.

Zoysia: In late March to April, apply a complete fertilizer such as 16-4-8, 16-0-8, or 32-0-16 with iron. In September, apply the same complete fertilizer again, or substitute 5-2-14 or similar winterizer.

Bermuda: In late March to April, apply a complete fertilizer such as 16-4-8, 16-0-8, or 32-0-16 with iron. Repeat in June and again in August or September. You could substitute 5-2-14 or similar winterizer for the September application.

THATCH AND SPONGY LAWNS

If your lawn seems very spongy when you walk across it, you may have an accumulation of thatch. Essentially, thatch is just an accumulation of old grass growth, mostly stems and runners, that have not decomposed. Many people mistakenly think that the clippings from mowing contribute to thatch. However, clippings, being high in moisture content, decompose fairly rapidly and do not contribute significantly to thatch.

The problem with thatch is that the grass, as it grows, tends to root in the thatch layer rather than the soil. Consequently, the grass becomes shallow-rooted and is prone to drought damage, cold damage, and many other problems.

To address severe thatch problems, many people "sand" their lawn in the spring. Topsoil, as weed-free as possible, spread in a very thin layer over the grass, is preferable to sand because it matches your existing soil.

To help prevent thatch problems from reaching the severe stage, consider having your lawn aerated annually by a lawn service with a heavy-duty core-type aerator. See the first section of this chapter on "Soil Conditions" for more of the benefits of aeration. The aeration may be done more than once a year if necessary. Avoid aeration during the winter, though.

For the most extreme cases of thatch, you may

have no choice except to have the lawn de-thatched. This involves using a machine with properly spaced vertical blades (too close a spacing will take out too much grass) to physically rip out the thatch. Huge amounts of thatch will be removed with this method and will have to be hauled off. It's a big job that you probably would be advised to have a lawn service perform. Many, though, don't have the proper machines or the desire to tackle such a time-consuming job.

If you decide to have your lawn de-thatched, it is imperative that the machine blades be spaced properly. If the blades are spaced too closely together too much grass will be removed and the lawn will be severely damaged. Set the blades at the following spaces: Bermuda and zoysia grasses...one to two inches; Centipede grass...two to three inches; Bahia and St. Augustine grasses...three inches.

But you can slow the accumulation of thatch by avoiding use of high water-soluble nitrogen fertilizers (see the section of the chapter on fertilizing) and by not watering and fertilizing more often than absolutely necessary.

Bermuda, zoysia, and bahia grasses have underground runners that enable them to come back even if much of the top of the grass is removed. But, if too many of the above-ground runners of centipede and St. Augustine grasses are removed, the lawn may die. Centipede and St. Augustine grasses have no underground runners from which to regenerate.

April is the best time to de-thatch a lawn. But it can be done as late in the growing season as July and still allow the lawn enough time to fill back in before frost.

In summary, save de-thatching as a last resort. It's a very involved job and it can remove tremendous amounts of your lawn. Do all that you can to prevent thatch and avoid the job of de-thatching.

Thatch just tends to accumulate in older lawns. And certain grasses, such as bermuda, zoysia, and St. Augustine grass tend to thatch more heavily than do centipede or bahia. But the key to keeping thatch from accumulating to troublesome levels is avoiding use of high water-soluble nitrogen fertilizers, by not fertilizing too often (see the section of this chapter on fertilizing), and by not watering more often than absolutely necessary.

NEMATODE PESTS

Nematodes are tiny (have to have a microscope to see them) roundworms that live in the soil. Certain kinds are harmful to certain grasses because they suck juices from the roots and stunt and otherwise damage root growth. This, of course, results in thinning of the lawn.

Control of nematodes is not that easy, though. Nematicides legal for home use are few, and the number of effective ones is even fewer. The key to dealing with nematodes lies in managing your grass to tolerate the nematodes rather than trying to eliminate them. That would be futile. Proper care is the first step to such management (the kind of care outlined in this chapter); but sometimes you can use other tricks like switching to a different type of grass that the particular nematode doesn't prefer.

The only way to find out how many nematodes and what kinds you have in your lawn is to have a laboratory sample run. Your local county cooperative extension service office can provide you with information about sending a sample of your lawn for a lab check. Once you receive the results back from the lab, you'll have to decide whether there are more management tricks you can use to handle the nematodes in your lawn or whether you will have to call in a lawn service licensed to perform pest control. A chemical nematicide treatment will temporarily reduce the nematode population but will provide no permanent solution. Only management works for the long term, though the nematicide can sometimes help give the lawn a little boost to get started again.

DISEASES

There are three conditions that must be met in order for a plant disease to occur. First, there must be a host plant. Second, there must be a disease-causing pathogen. Third, there must be favorable environmental conditions for the disease to develop.

In the case of lawn diseases, two of those conditions are always present. The host plant, your lawn, is always there. And, believe it or not, in most cases, the fungal pathogen is almost always present,

too - either in the soil or in the thatch layer. The only factor that remains to be provided is a favorable environment in terms of moisture and temperature. Once that favorable environment is provided, the fungus can start growing, attacking the plant, and spreading.

Most fungus diseases are favored by prolonged periods of moisture. Don't water the lawn more than is necessary. And when you water, it's best to water early in the morning - so that the grass surface stays wet no longer than necessary. Set your sprinkler system to come on at 2:00 or 3:00 a.m. and go off about the time you get up. Or, if you're using a hose and sprinkler, try to start the water as soon as you get up and turn it off as you leave for work. Or, you can buy an inexpensive timer that will turn the water off for you.

As long as environmental conditions favor fungal spread, stopping a disease will be difficult, especially if the thatch layer in the lawn is thick. That's why it is so important to reduce thatch buildup by not over-fertilizing and over-watering.

Disease severity will be enhanced, too, if the grass is under stress from being mowed too low. So, be careful not to add this stress to your lawn. When a disease is active is the one time you should bag the clippings when you mow. Mow the diseased area last so as not to track fungus spores to the other part of the lawn. And, use the bagger to catch the clippings from the diseased area.

Don't think that spraying a fungicide will eradicate a lawn disease and keep it from coming back. Fungicides don't kill the fungi that cause lawn diseases. They can only force the fungus into a state of temporary dormancy - provided you obtain good coverage, don't have too heavy a thatch layer, use the proper fungicide, and use proper timing. Repeat applications may be necessary to keep the fungus dormant long enough for the grass to regain its strength. The long-term solution to managing lawn diseases, though, lies in keeping the grass healthy and not providing the ideal conditions for development of the fungus. Otherwise, spraying will only provide temporary relief.

When a fungus disease is active, it will usually spread fast. If you have a dead spot in your lawn that stays the same size for weeks, chances are the fungus is no longer active there and a fungicide application would do no good. If, on the other hand, the trouble spot is rapidly becoming larger over a period of a week or so, then it is a good possibility that you have an active fungus problem. Search for insect pests first, though, and rule them out.

There are several fungicides that can be used to stop the spread of fungus diseases in a lawn. But not all of the fungicides control all of the diseases. Your garden center should have some basic fungicides in small packages, such as Daconil 2787, that will help with some of the diseases. But, many lawn fungicides only come in larger packages such as licensed pest control operators would buy.

If you choose to have a pest control company spray the diseased area, be sure that the company has the necessary licensing and that the applicator has a card specifying licensure.

In summary, the key to disease control is providing the lawn with its basic needs but not over-watering, over-fertilizing, and mowing too low. Also, water at the proper time so as not to keep the lawn overly moist. Fungicides will only provide temporary relief.

INSECT PESTS

While there are normally always a few pest insects in any lawn, they aren't there in damaging numbers. The vast majority of insects in a lawn tend to be either harmless or beneficial.

To check for pest insects in a trouble spot in your lawn, get on your hands and knees and look closely near the soil line at the borders of the trouble spot. Remember, you're only concerned with pest insects; many of the others you see will be either harmless insects or even beneficial insects and spiders. If you don't easily see pests, you may try a soapy water flush that will drive many insects, good and bad, out of the thatch or soil. Mix an ounce of dishwashing detergent with two gallons of water. Slowly drench the mixture over a 2 x 2 ft. area. Watch for several minutes.

Spittlebugs are small (about 1/4 inch) dark brown to black insects with two orange stripes across their back. Their underside is also orange. They frequently become a problem on lush centipede grass in mid to late summer as they suck on the grass plants and discolor them. Typically, they cause a yellow or red streaking of the grass blades. Other types of grasses aren't normally damaged.

Chinch bugs are tiny black insects (about 1/16 to 1/8 inch) with white patches on the tops of their wing pads. The even tinier immatures are red. Chinch bugs stay near the soil line, sucking on the St. Augustine grass plants, usually in sunny areas of the lawn. They do not affect the other types of lawn grasses; only St. Augustine grass is affected.

Chinch bug feeding results in yellowed areas of the lawn that turn straw-colored with time. A good way to check for chinch bugs in the lawn is to dig several clumps of sod from the perimeter of declining areas. Shake the grass over a white paper plate. If you shake well, and if chinch bugs are present, they should be more easily seen as they fall to the plate.

Mole crickets are tan to brown insects with rounded heads and short, stubby legs for digging. They don't hop like field crickets, but they do crawl rapidly as they dig through the soil eating grass roots and making their slightly raised tunnels in the soil.

Sod webworm damage is not very common in our area. It is usually late summer when it starts. In early stages, a close examination will reveal that grass blades have been chewed. If the damage becomes very severe (and it can—very rapidly), about all that remains will be grass runners. If you look very closely around the soil line you may find some of the quarter inch long caterpillars curled in a C-shape. The light green caterpillars are nocturnal and rest during the day, so they're often hard to find. You also may find small piles of excrement if you look very closely. Often, the tan-colored adult moths can be seen flitting around the lawn during the day.

Just because you find a few of any of these insects does not mean that you have an insect problem in your lawn. Make sure that you have sufficient numbers to warrant treatment. You'll never completely eradicate any type of insects from your lawn and it is futile to try. Only when you have a large number causing visible damage in a spot is treatment necessary. And, then, you can often just

> *J*ust because you find a few of any of these insects does not mean that you have an insect problem in your lawn.

treat the infested area and about a 15 ft. border around it. Sometimes, though, the infestation will spread and the whole lawn will have to be treated. Monitor the infestation closely.

Be sure you use an insecticide that is labeled for the particular insect you are attempting to control. Ask the nursery or garden center personnel for recommendations. But take it on yourself to read the label before you leave the nursery to make sure the product is really the one you want. For caterpillars,

Chinch bugs can be a problem in St. Augustine grass. And, spittlebugs are a common problem in centipede grass.

try to use an insecticide containing *Bacillus thuringiensis*. BT, as it is sometimes called, is a bacterium that kills only caterpillars. It will not harm the beneficial insects

and spiders that feed on the pest insects in your lawn.

SPRING LAWN PROBLEMS

Every spring many people complain of dead spots as many of the factors outlined already in this chapter. Fungus disease during the winter, drought during the winter, etc. can be factors, especially if compounded by a weak root system and a cold winter. Even a completely healthy lawn can sometimes be killed in spots by cold when that cold is in spring or late winter and preceded by a warm spell that caused the grass to begin growing early. Be sure to water your lawn during dry periods in the winter to prevent drought damage. The roots still need water. Don't let the soil become excessively dry.

Some spring yellowing is usually not caused by disease, but rather by iron chlorosis. A little iron, available from your nursery or garden center, may quickly turn the lawn back to a healthy green. It will usually turn green on its own, though, given a couple of weeks. The iron chlorosis is difficult to explain but seems to have something to do with the grass forming new roots in the spring and the cool soil temperatures. Many times the problem is aggravated by early spring fertilization. It is advisable to wait until 3 weeks after the grass greens up to fertilize. Make sure the fertilizer is something similar to a 16-4-8 with 8% water-insoluble nitrogen.

Regardless how bad your lawn looks in the early spring, give it some time. To be patient is the best advice I can give you. Don't fertilize until after danger of frost, around mid-March. Then give the fertilizer about a month to work. Water deeply if the weather is dry but water only as often as needed to keep the grass from wilting.

If, after fertilizing, watering as needed, and giving the lawn about a month, it still has dead areas, you may need to replant the larger dead areas which appear to have no live grass left in them. But, first, give time, the weather, fertilizer, and water a chance to help.

In summary, patience is the best remedy for many of the spring lawn problems. Given time and a little basic care such as mowing, fertilizing, and watering, chances are that your lawn will grow out of most of its spring patchiness. Spraying with fungicides in the early spring is not likely to help because there is usually no disease active then.

WEEDS IN THE LAWN

You'll always have a few weeds in your lawn. It's nothing to get overly alarmed about. If you just take good care of your grass, it will usually choke the weeds out with time.

Many of the weeds are annual weeds, anyway, and only live for one season before going to seed and dying. They'll sprout back up the next fall or spring, depending on whether they're winter or summer annuals, and you'll not be troubled by them again until then.

You have several options for controlling these annual weeds. The best option is usually to apply a pre-emergence herbicide just before time for the seed to germinate (usually in late October for winter

In summary, patience is the best remedy for many of the spring lawn problems. Given time and a little basic care such as mowing, fertilizing, and watering, chances are that your lawn will grow out of most of its spring patchiness. Spraying with fungicides in the early spring is not likely to help because there is usually no disease active then.

weeds or mid-March for summer weeds). But, there are also post-emergent herbicides that can be applied after the weed is already up to try and kill the full-grown weed.

The problem with any herbicide application to lawns is that it is risky business. If you calibrate the sprayer incorrectly, apply too much or the wrong herbicide over an area, or apply on a windy day, you could severely damage your lawn or shrubs. Believe me, it happens all the time!

It's best to leave herbicide application to professionals who have plenty of experience. Make sure that they are licensed by the state to perform lawn and ornamental pest control. Ask to see their card.

If you choose to apply a herbicide yourself, you'll probably only find several lawn herbicides available for use on lawns by home gardeners. Atrazine, a common pre-emergent herbicide, available in liquid form and also available in many weed-and-feed fertilizers, gives good control of some weeds that have already emerged in some types of grasses. There are also post-emergent herbicides consisting of several possible combinations of 2,4-D, dicamba, or MCPP, but be very careful with them. It's safest not to use them on St. Augustine. Depending on your locale, you may find additional herbicides with specifics depending on the type of grass you have.

> *The problem with any herbicide application to lawns is that it is risky business. If you calibrate the sprayer incorrectly, apply too much or the wrong herbicide over an area, or apply on a windy day, you could severely damage your lawn or shrubs. Believe me, it happens all the time!*

Before using a herbicide, read the herbicide label thoroughly and follow it to the letter. In fact, read the label before you even buy the herbicide to make sure you're buying the correct product for your type of lawn grass and the weeds involved. Don't blindly trust the sales person. No one herbicide can be used on all types of grasses.

PLANTING A NEW LAWN

Depending on the type of lawn, as mentioned at the beginning of this chapter, lawns can be started from seed, sod, sprigs, or plugs. Bahia and centipede are the only lawns you're likely to start from seed.

Most lawns will either be started from sod or plugs. *Sprigs*, which are individual stems or pieces of stem that have the potential to root, are not used that often, except for starting bermuda grass, and possibly zoysia grass lawns. Sprigs are usually broadcast over a prepared soil and then pressed into the soil with a sod roller. An alternative method is to plant the sprigs end to end in furrows six to twelve inches apart. The sprigs are covered with an inch or two of soil, leaving part of each sprig exposed to the light. The furrow method is usually used for zoysia grass, whereas the broadcast method is usually used for bermuda grass.

Sodding, though appearing on the surface to be the way to an instant lawn, is not completely fool-proof. The sod pieces, having a thin root system, must regenerate a new, deep root system. Care of the sod during the period until new roots are formed is critical.

Before laying sod, thoroughly rototill the area and rake the soil surface clean. Thoroughly moisten the soil. Lay the sod pieces in a staggered brick-like pattern with the edges fitted tightly together to avoid any open cracks. If there are cracks, fill them with soil.

After the sod is laid, fertilize as you would an existing lawn. Water the sod until it is thoroughly moistened. Then roll the sod with a sod roller to ensure close contact with the soil.

> *Be sure that the site on which you intend to plant the sod is sunny enough and well drained enough. If you have any doubts, the only way to assure that the site is suitable is to put out a small test patch of the grass first.*

Water the sod at least twice a day. Water in mid to late morning and again in mid afternoon with only enough water to thoroughly moisten the sod pieces and to begin to moisten the soil below. You don't want the sod to become sopping wet. But you must not allow the roots to dry out either.

Once the sod roots knit down into the soil below, you can reduce watering to an as needed basis. Still, don't allow the grass to become wilted for long periods. Once the grass turns the wilted gray-green color, turn on the water.

BUYING SOD

When you buy sod, naturally you will consider price. But don't ignore other factors such as percentage of weeds contained, presence of pest insects, or diseases. Is the sod cut with a generous layer of soil and roots, or does it tear apart easily as you handle it because it is cut too thin? How long does the sod sit on the pallet after it is cut and before it is planted? Sod life on pallets during summer is less than 48 hours. Generally, how does the sod look? If it looks dry, weedy, or diseased before you plant it, don't expect it to get better. It may, but if it doesn't you may very well be stuck with it. When buying plants, and especially when buying lawn grass sod, it's wise for the consumer to remember the old caveat emptor, let the buyer beware.

Other problems in establishing a lawn from sod are often attributable to the site selection, site preparation, or care of the sod after planting. The site may be too shaded to grow lawn grass. The soil may have been inadequately tilled and may be too compacted. The sod may have dried out for just one sunny day after planting when the air temperature was 95 degrees. Or, as is sometimes the case, the sod may have been kept too saturated and a fungus disease began to rot it. Insect pests, too, can get started after the sod is laid.

There are just so many factors that can be involved in the failure of a lawn to establish successfully from sod that it is very difficult to pinpoint

Remember when you see lawn grass advertisements in newspapers or magazines that advertisements are intended to cause the consumer to want to buy the advertised product. A wise consumer must realize that any claims as to the performance of the product are always subject to certain unspecified but implied limitations.

who is at fault. So, even if you feel that you have justifiably placed the blame of a sod failure on the sod vendor, you may have little recourse to force the vendor to refund your money or replace the sod.

You need to be an informed customer when buying sod. Be sure that the site on which you intend to plant the sod is sunny enough and well-drained enough. If you have any doubts, the only way to assure that the site is suitable is to put out a small test patch of the grass first. Give it a month or so to see how it performs. Does it spread? Or does it look worse as time goes on. You may be impatient or feel confident in sodding the whole area without running such a test. But just be aware that it is your risk and yours alone.

Make sure that the sod is of a type of lawn grass suited for your site. Much 'Floratam' is sold in north Florida because it is the most readily available St. Augustine grass cultivar in Florida. Therefore, it is usually available for the lowest price. But, beware that University of Florida Extension turfgrass specialists rate 'Floratam' St. Augustine grass as having poor cold tolerance and poor shade tolerance. Other St. Augustine grass cultivars such as 'Seville', 'Delmar', 'Jade', 'Raleigh', and 'Bitter Blue' are classified as having at least good cold tolerance and good shade tolerance. But these grasses are in less supply and often are considerably more expensive than is 'Floratam'. You, as a consumer, have to decide whether you're willing to pay more for the shade and cold tolerances of these other grasses.

Remember when you see lawn grass advertisements in newspapers or magazines that advertisements are intended to cause the consumer to want to buy the advertised product. A wise consumer must realize that any claims as to the performance of the product are always subject to certain unspecified but implied limitations.

A little extra effort and expense is involved in carefully shopping for sod, carefully preparing the site for planting, and giving it attentive care once planted. But considering the hundreds or thousands of dollars you're spending on the sod, it's well worth the effort and extra expense.

USING PLUGS TO PLANT A NEW LAWN OR REPAIR A DAMAGED LAWN

Using plugs to plant a lawn is not a new idea.

People have been using plugs the hard way for years, cutting the plugs themselves from sod pieces. But the introduction of nursery-grown grass plugs a few years back has made it easier than ever to plant from plugs. Nursery-grown plugs are especially useful in repairing small areas of damage in your lawn.

Nursery-grown plugs have several advantages over plugs cut from sod. First, you skip the dirty task of having to chop plugs from a piece of sod with a machete or hatchet. Instead, you simply pull the plugs out of a tray. The trays, by the way, are a lot less messy to haul home in the trunk of your car than is sod.

Plugs cut from sod have a shallow root system that was disrupted from the field when the sod was cut. But plugs grown in a tray at a nursery have a well-established root system, 2-3 inches deep, that is actively growing. The plugs go through no transplanting shock. Planting sod, or plugs from sod, is similar to transplanting a tree from one field site to another. There is a certain amount of transplant shock and a critical period of root regeneration.

If necessary, plugs in trays can be held for weeks before planting. In the summer, sod can normally be held no longer than 48 hours after it is cut from the sod field.

As you might guess, nursery-grown plugs are much more expensive than are plugs you cut from sod yourself. A tray of 18 four-inch plugs typically costs $5-$6. A square foot of sod is priced in the range of 20-50 cents and should yield 9 four-inch plugs. So, for 40 cents to a dollar, you could buy 18 plugs worth of sod. You'll have to factor in the advantages of an established root system, the convenience, and the ease of planting to decide if nursery-grown plugs are the right choice for you.

If your soil is soft and workable, it is easy to plant plugs. Basically, you just dig a hole and plant the plug as you would a flower plant or any other type of plant. Available at garden centers are even plugging tools that dig perfectly sized holes for the plugs. But, you can use a shovel or a garden trowel also, especially if the soil is hard and compacted and needs a little cultivation. Space the plugs twelve to eighteen inches apart.

After planting, fertilize and water. Be sure that the plugs receive water, either from rain or irrigation, every day for about two weeks. Then reduce the frequency of watering to about every other day for a month. After this period, water only as needed.

Planting grass plugs is a good way to fill in damaged areas of the lawn without having to till up the whole area to plant sod. If the soil is very hard, though, it is advisable to till up the whole area, even when using plugs. Otherwise, the plugs will not easily spread over the hard soil.

Planting a few plugs in a shaded area where you wish to grow grass is an inexpensive way to see if the area receives enough sunlight to grow grass. if the plugs don't spread within a month or so, it could be a good indication that you shouldn't invest further money in grass for the area.

PLANTING RYE GRASS FOR WINTER COLOR OR EROSION CONTROL

During most winters the top growth of our permanent lawn grasses goes dormant and turns brown. To maintain a green lawn during the winter you can overseed your permanent lawn with a cool-season lawn grass. Annual, intermediate, and perennial (improved) rye grasses may be used.

The rye grass will grow through the winter and die in the heat of the following spring. It has to be reseeded each year.

Other than for aesthetics or erosion control in bare areas, there are no practical reasons for overseeding with rye grass. In fact, rye grass and your permanent grass will compete somewhat for nutrients, water, and sunlight in the early spring when the permanent grass is emerging but before the rye grass dies. To discourage this competition, and to hasten the transition from rye grass back to permanent grass, don't fertilize the rye grass after January. Water as infrequently as possible. Keep the rye grass mowed closely during late winter and early spring.

When seeding rye grass in the fall, wait until daytime temperatures are fairly consistently in the 70's. This should be late October to November.

Mow your lawn closely, either bagging clippings or raking clippings after mowing. Spread the rye grass seed with a cyclone seed spreader. Overseed with annual or intermediate type rye grasses at 5-10 lbs. of seed per 1,000 square feet of lawn. Use 10-20 lbs. for perennial type rye grasses. When seeding bare ground with annual rye grass, use a rate of about 10 lbs. per 1,000 sq. ft.

Perennial ryes will not act as perennials in our climate. One of their advantages over annual rye is that they will die more quickly and evenly in the spring as the permanent grass is resuming growth, making for a smoother transition.

Water the lawn once or twice a day until the rye grass seeds have germinated. Continue watering until the seedlings are well-established. Don't water so much as to cause puddles because they will wash the seed away. Also, over-watering will encourage disease development. Once the lawn is established, only water as needed.

Weekly mowing will be required. Don't fertilize until after the lawn has been mowed several times. Fertilize with 16-4-8 fertilizer (containing 8% water-insoluble nitrogen) at the rate of 3-4 lbs. per 1,000 square feet. Fertilize monthly through January. You may decide overseeding with rye grass is not worth the trouble. Or, you may decide just to overseed a small highly visible area rather than overseed your entire lawn.

8

Groundcovers

Alternatives to Lawn grasses

Groundcovers are low-growing plants used to cover areas in the landscape much as a lawn is used. The primary advantage groundcovers have over a lawn, though, is that groundcovers are much easier to maintain once established. Groundcovers don't require weekly mowing or frequent fertilization and watering.

There are added advantages, too. Groundcovers are attractive because they add varying textures and colors to the landscape and reduce the boring sameness of too much lawn. Groundcovers will often grow in areas not suited for lawn grasses. For instance, there are many goundcovers suitable for shaded areas and groundcovers suited for areas too steep to be mowed.

Groundcovers, however, will not replace lawn areas intended for recreational purposes or widespread traffic. Restricted traffic can be handled in groundcover areas with the use of stepping stones or mulched paths. But groundcovers cannot replace a lawn for activities such as children's play.

STARTING GROUNDCOVER PLANTINGS

The most difficult part of growing groundcovers is the establishment period. Cost of plants can be a problem. But cost can often be reduced by obtaining plants from friends with an established groundcover area in need of thinning or edging.

Planting a bed of groundcover can be tiring, too,

because it often involves planting a number of very small plants. Sometimes it even involves dividing the plants to be planted into smaller divisions.

Before planting, rototill the whole area to be planted. If there are weeds present, ideally, one or two applications of Roundup® or other such glyphosate herbicide should be applied several weeks or several months before rototilling. This will give the herbicide time to work, and in the case of two applications, a chance to kill weeds that are likely to re-sprout from the first application.

If you rototill with live weeds still in the bed, you may or may not have significant future weed problems, depending on the type of weed present. Your best bet is to allow time to use the glyphosate herbicide if possible. Even doing so, you'll probably have to pull some weeds the first couple of years, until the groundcovers in the bed grow in full and thick. A mulch of pine straw or other such organic material during the establishment period will help reduce weed sprouting. Don't use landscape weed fabrics because they will interfere with the spread of your groundcover unless your groundcover is a type such as juniper that doesn't spread by runners or sprouts from roots.

Water and fertilization, such as with a newly established lawn, will be important during the establishment period.

*G*roundcovers are low-growing plants used to cover areas in the landscape much as a lawn is used. The primary advantage groundcovers have over a lawn, though, is that groundcovers are much easier to maintain once established. Groundcovers don't require weekly mowing or frequent fertilization and watering.

Once well-established, most groundcovers are fairly low in required maintenance. However, you may have to trim the planting to keep it from encroaching into unwanted areas. And, some groundcovers, such as liriope, may get old, spotted leaves that need annual trimming before the spring growth emerges from the base. With liriope, simply remove the old growth at a point just above the newly emerging leaves in late winter or very early spring.

GROUNDCOVERS FOR SUN OR PARTIAL SHADE

Ajuga reptans
Daylily (*Hemerocallis spp.*)
Lioriope muscari
Blue phlox (*Phlox divaricata*)
Moss phlox (*Phlox subulata*)
Asiatic jasmine (*Trachelospermum asiaticum*)

GROUNDCOVERS FOR FULL SUN

Shore juniper (*Juniperus conferta*)
Creeping juniper (*Juniperus horizontalis*):
    includes 'Bar Harbor', 'Blue Rug', etc.
Japanese garden juniper (*Juniperus procumbens*)

GROUNDCOVERS FOR SHADE OR PARTIAL SHADE

Ajuga reptans
Creeping ardisia (*Ardisia japonica*)
Aspidistra or cast-iron plant (*Aspidistra elatior*)
Goldenstar or green & gold (*Chrysogonum virginianum*)
Holly fern (*Cyrtomium falcatum*)
Dwarf gardenia (*Gardenia jasminoides* 'Radicans' or 'Prostrata')
Algerian ivy (*Hedera canariensis*)
English ivy (*Hedera helix*)

Hosta spp.
Liriope muscari
Creeping liriope (*Liriope spicata*)
Mondo grass, including dwarf Mondo grass (*Ophiopogon japonicus*)
Wood fern (*Thelypteris normalis*) and other native ferns
Asiatic jasmine (*Trachelospermum asiaticum*)
Periwinkle (*Vinca minor* or *Vinca major*)

FERTILIZING GROUNDCOVERS

Once groundcovers are well established and healthy-looking, you can usually quit fertilizing them. Fertilizer may sometimes be needed, though, in sandy soils or to help plantings recover from some type of damage. If you do fertilize, use about a cup of 16-4-8 per 100 sq. ft. in March and possibly again in July. Fertilization is important in the establishment period when you are trying to make the groundcover planting fill in.

~ Color for All Seasons ~
Late Winter and Early Spring Color

Photo by David W. Marshall

ABOVE: Taiwan cherry is one of our earliest flowering ornamental cherry trees, usually flowering in February. It's a fast grower and extremely popular. Seedlings that sprout beneath trees can easily be transplanted to start new trees.

RIGHT: The Japanese magnolia, *Magnolia soulangiana*, is typically a February flowering tree. Flowers sometimes can be harmed by hard winter freezes, but usually, North Florida winters are mild enough to cause no serious problems.

Photo by David W. Marshall

Photo by Gary Knox

ABOVE: 'Ann' is a new hybrid magnolia from a series called the 'Little Girl Hybrids', developed at the National Arboretum. It flowers in late winter.

LEFT: Bridalwreath spirea, a deciduous shrub, makes a spectacular early spring-flowering hedge. It flowers about the same time as the azaleas.

Photo by David W. Marshall

RIGHT: The fringe trees *Chionanthus virginicus* (grandaddy greybeard) and *C. retusus* are very reliable, small, spring-flowering trees.

Photo by David W. Marshall

RIGHT: 'Welch Junior Miss' is the only pink dogwood proven so far to do well in our climatic zone. It doesn't flower as well as the white dogwoods after very mild winters, though.

Photo by David W. Marshall

~ Late Spring & Summer Color ~

Some to include in a butterfly garden . . .

Photo by David W. Marshall/Inset by Steve Cannon

ABOVE: The tall plant on the right is *Buddleia Davidii*, butterfly bush. It is an excellent shrubby perennial for color from late spring until frost. It's very attractive to butterflies. The lower-growing lavender and pink flowers on the left are *Verbena canadensis*. The inset is of a different butterfly bush cultivar, illustrating that there are different colors available.

Photo by David W. Marshall

ABOVE: Lantana is one of our toughest, most drought-tolerant perennials. It's also one of our best butterfly plants. Lantana is available in several different colors and sizes.

Photo by David W. Marshall

TOP: Pentas, the pink flowers in the background, are an extremely reliable flower for sun to partial shade. Attractive to hummingbirds and butterflies, pentas also come in red and white. Further south or in protected areas here, they may be considered as perennials. Society garlic is the blue plant in the foreground.

RIGHT: Don't forget garden zinnias as an easy-to-grow from seed annual. Because of their attractiveness to butterflies, they're used here in the butterfly garden at Callaway Gardens in Georgia. Growing zinnias from seed is an easy gardening project for children.

Photo by David W. Marshall

~ *Tough, reliable annuals for summer's heat . . .* ~

Photo by David W. Marshall

Photo by David W. Marshall

ABOVE: Globe amaranth, *Gomphrena globosa*, is one of our better summer annuals, being fairly tolerant of our heat and humidity. The flowers can be used in arrangements or for drying. There are also dwarf types and red types.

LEFT: *Zinnia angustifolia*, (formerly *Z. linearis*), is an extremely tough, low-growing, drought-tolerant annual that tolerates our harsh summers well. Flowers are yellow-orange, but there is also a white form.

Photo by David W. Marshall

ABOVE: *Melampodium paludosum* is a rapidly growing annual that is very well-suited for the high heat and humidity of our summers. It will even tolerate a little shade. 'Medallion' and 'Showstar' are popular cultivars. Each small plant can grow to a 2 ft. height and a 2 ft. spread. Melampodium also re-seeds prolifically.

RIGHT: Ornamental peppers should not be forgotten as a way to add color to the garden.

Photo by David W. Marshall

~ Very reliable perennials . . . ~

Photo by David W. Marshall/Inset by Steve Cannon

ABOVE: *Salvia* x 'Indigo Spires' is probably our best perennial salvia. It produces long spikes of blue-purple flowers from late spring until frost. Lantana is at the top left and *Rudbeckia*, 'Goldsturm' is at the lower left.

Photo by David W. Marshall/Inset by Steve Cannon

LEFT: *Salvia guaranitica* is a blue-flowering perennial that flowers from early summer until frost. There is also a violet-flowering form, shown in the inset. This salvia spreads in clumps.

Photo by David W. Marshall

RIGHT: Purple coneflower, *Echinacea purpurea*, is an easy-to-grow native perennial for sun to partial shade. It is very attractive to butterflies when grown in full sun.

Photo by David W. Marshall

LEFT: Plumbago is a shrubby perennial for full sun to partial shade. It flowers from early summer through fall. Plumbago grows quite large. There is only one plumbago plant in this photo.

LEFT: *Rudbeckia fulgida*, 'Goldsturm', is the most popular of the rudbeckias. It is a summer- to fall-blooming perennial for the full sun.

Photo by David W. Marshall

RIGHT: *Justicia carnea*, jacobinia, is not well known, but is a wonderful perennial for shaded gardens. It flowers from early summer until frost. Anyone with a shaded yard should have some justicia.

Photo by David W. Marshall

Photo by David W. Marshall

ABOVE: *Hibiscus coccineus* is a perennial hibiscus native to swampy areas in Florida and Georgia. It freezes to the ground in winter but flowers well in summer and fall.

~ Fall Color. . . Perennials ~

RIGHT: Mexican sage, *Salvia leucantha*, is a reliable fall-blooming salvia liked by hummingbirds. This particular selection has flowers of all purple. Purple and white flowers are more common as shown in the inset.

Photo by David W. Marshall/Inset by Steve Cannon

Photo by David W. Marshall

RIGHT: Philippine violet, *Barleria cristata*, produces beautiful purple flowers in October and November. The plant is a perennial but is not well known yet. It's easy to grow and comes back each spring after winter freezes.

Photo by David W. Marshall

LEFT: Cigar flower, *Cuphea micropetala*, is a tough, drought-tolerant perennial that flowers in the fall. Plant height is typically 3-4 feet. For full sun.

Photo by David W. Marshall

ABOVE: Firespike, *Odontonema strictum*, is a perennial that produces bright red tubular flowers, popular with hummingbirds, in the fall. It prefers partial shade or filtered sunlight.

Photo by David W. Marshall

ABOVE: *Chrysanthemum* x 'Mei-kyo', is a perennial mum that produces numerous small pink flowers in fall. It grows well and spreads rapidly. Pineapple sage (*Salvia elegans*) another fall-blooming perennial, on the right, is popular with hummingbirds.

Photo by David W. Marshall

LEFT: Swamp sunflower is a tall sunflower that produces brilliant yellow flowers in October, drawing attention away from everything else in the garden. Because of its height and growth rate, it may need staking.

Photo by David W. Marshall

~ Trees . . . ~

RIGHT: The Bradford pear, because of its fall color, is one of our most popular street trees. It has white spring flowers, but it doesn't flower heavily here after mild winters.

RIGHT: Though the live oak is very popular in our zone, the deciduous oaks, such as the white oak, shown here, provide fall color and allow the sun's warming rays to penetrate in the winter. Not shading in the winter, the deciduous oaks also allow more sunlight for growing winter annuals, such as pansies, or early spring flowers, such as sweet peas. Shumard oak is another deciduous oak that provides even better fall color, a beautiful red.

Photo by David W. Marshall

LEFT: Few trees can match the golden fall color of the ginkgo tree. It's a slow-growing tree that prefers moist, fertile, but well-drained soil.

Photo by David W. Marshall

~ *Plant these in fall for early spring color . . .* ~

Photo by David W. Marshall

ABOVE: *Dianthus*, 'First Love', a relatively new dianthus, has performed beautifully in local trials. It flowers well in fall, winter and spring and has a nice, delicate fragrance

Photo by David W. Marshall

ABOVE: Poppies, such as these California poppies, are winter annuals that should be planted in late October or November. They bloom in late winter and early spring. The winter cold won't hurt them.

10
Flowers

Liven the Landscape with Color

The use of flowers in home landscapes is more popular than ever before. Garden catalogs and magazines bombard us with new variety after new variety of flower. Never before have we had such choices of flowers for our landscapes!

But all the choices can be more than a little confusing for even the experienced gardener. Which flowers will grow well in our area and which will not?

Though I certainly don't have all the answers, either, I have been particularly interested in the subject of flowers. I've read extensively on the subject and have conducted many trials, putting many flowers to the test of the heat and humidity of Tallahassee's climate. While I haven't finished learning and don't have all the answers by any means, I pass along my findings, so far, to you in hopes that they'll be helpful.

I've divided this chapter into sections on:

1) *perennials* (those flowers that should live longer than one year), 2) *annuals* (those that live one season), and 3) *flowers that should be planted in the fall.* Too often gardeners miss out on these flowers because they forget to plant them.

GROWING PERENNIAL FLOWERS

Landscape trends come, go, and return over the years just as do trends in clothing. Years ago perennial flowers, such as shasta daisies, rudbeckias,

coreopsis, and phlox were found in many home gardens. Then came the tremendous surge of the use of flowering annuals.

But, as we've become more sophisticated gardeners, we've rediscovered that perennial flowers have their place in the garden, too. The fact that we don't have to replant perennials year after year is one of their most popular attributes. But, the joy of seeing perennials emerge, grow, flower, die back to the ground, and emerge again, year after year, helps to satisfy a certain need to see change and growth in the garden that lies within most gardeners.

WHEN TO PLANT PERENNIALS

Gardening with perennial flowers requires a different approach than does gardening with annuals, though. Growing most perennials requires a little more patience than does growing annuals. You need to plan ahead. You shouldn't wait until spring to plant perennials. Fall is a better time. And, when you buy perennials you shouldn't care so much about buying a plant with a bushy top and lots of flower buds as about buying a plant with a strong root system.

It's the root system that will carry the plant through the winter and push the strong growth upward next spring that will produce the flowers. The root system is the basis of all growth to come.

Some retail nurseries sell bare-root perennials in

One way to improve soil drainage, and a way that should probably be used much more often in growing perennials in our area, is to use raised beds.

the fall and winter. Buying bare-root perennials is one way you can save a few dollars when buying perennials. Because you're not buying pots and soil with the plants, they are less expensive than potted plants. When selecting bare-root perennials, look for an extensive root system and make sure the nursery has kept the roots fresh and moist.

A few plants considered perennials in the north perform more as annuals for us. A prime example is the delphinium. Delphiniums, noted for their tall spikes of flowers in varying shades of blue, just don't seem to like our hot, humid summers. Yet, if delphinium plants are set out in the fall, you can have a traffic-stopping show of color the following spring. They're worth planting as annuals if you can get the plants in fall.

SOIL PREPARATION FOR PERENNIALS

When planting perennials, as when planting most flowers, it is very important that you consider soil drainage. Many perennials will not survive long periods in soggy soil. Our high annual rainfall and our clay soils are probably responsible for many of the failures gardeners experience when trying to grow perennials.

One way to improve soil drainage, and a way that should probably be used much more often in growing perennials in our area, is to use raised beds. A raised bed improves drainage, but it also makes a great way to display the flowers because they're not all at the same height. It's a little like viewing the fall color of trees growing on the side of a mountain as opposed to viewing the fall color on a forest of trees at ground level.

You can make a raised bed by bringing in topsoil to raise the soil level. Mushroom compost or other organic matter might be used to mix with the topsoil. But don't use straight mushroom compost, peat, garden compost, or other such material without mixing it with topsoil, or it will hold too much moisture and defeat one of the primary purposes of

the raised bed.

Regardless whether you use a raised bed or not, cultivate this soil until it is friable before you plant. Whereas you can sometimes get by planting short-lived flowers in poorly prepared soil, remember that a perennial must live in the same spot for years.

FERTILIZING PERENNIALS

There's no across-the-board rule on fertilizing perennial flowers. Many, such as gaillardia, prefer almost no fertilizer. Other, though, could benefit from light fertilization periodically through the season. You can use the same 16-4-8 you use for your lawn, trees, and shrubs, IF it is composed of 8% water-insoluble or slow-release nitrogen. Otherwise, it's too high in nitrogen. Use about a cup per 100 sq. ft. for heavy-feeders. Reduce the rate accordingly for lighter feeders. Should you choose to use 8-8-8, use

There's no across-the-board rule on fertilizing perennial flowers. Some, such as gaillardia, prefer almost no fertilizer.

about 1 ¾ cups for the heavy feeders. Avoid getting fertilizer on the plants themselves. If fertilizer does get on the plants, wash it off. Fertilizing in early March, late June, and again in August should be sufficient for most.

SOME PERENNIALS YOU MAY WISH TO TRY

Agapanthus or African lily (Agapanthus africanus): Clusters of blue flowers are borne atop tall stems during summer to fall. For sunny, well-drained sites.

Butterfly weed (Asclepias tuberosa): Drought-tolerant native, often seen among the grasses on roadsides. orange flowers. Some cultivars available with yellow flowers. Flowers May-September. For sunny spots.

Aster laevis: This seems to be the most reliable and showiest aster for the Tallahassee area. The small lavender flowers with yellow centers appear throughout much of the spring, summer, and fall. I've had a planting live from year to year for six years now. The only drawback to this plant is that it gets a little leggy and may need some staking. Height is about eighteen inches. Full sun.

Phillipine violet (Barleria cristata): An attractive plant, reaching four feet or so over the course of the growing season. Beautiful purple flowers cover the plant in October and November. The winter cold may burn the plant to the ground, but it comes back next spring. Full sun to partial shade.

Butterfly bush (Buddleia spp.): A shrubby perennial reaching 10 ft. or so tall. Bears flower spikes in shades of purple, blue, or pink, attractive to butterflies. For sun to light shade.

Chrysanthemum (Chrysanthemum morifolium): Fall-blooming perennial. Pinch until mid-August to induce business. Various traditional fall colors of golds, oranges, yellows, etc. For sun.

Korean mum (Chrysanthemum hybrid): Pink-flowering fall chrysanthemum. Pinch until mid-August to induce bushiness. For sun.

Chrysanthemum x 'Mei-kyo': Small, one-inch flowers of dark rose with yellow centers in October. Keep pinched until mid-August to induce bushiness. Very vigorous grower and heavy flowerer. I first found this plant at Holbrook Farm in Fletcher, N.C. A relative newcomer to the United States. For sun.

Shasta daisy (Chrysanthemum x superbum): Old garden favorite. White flowers with yellow centers. 'May Queen' seems to be one particularly good cultivar. Flowers late spring to early summer. Sun.

Sweet autumn clematis (Clematis dioscorifolia): Fall-blooming clematis becomes covered with small, white, fragrant flowers. Very easy to grow, is sometimes considered to be a native, though it was actually introduced to our area. Sun, light shade.

Coreopsis (Coreopsis spp.): Several species of this yellow summer-flowering perennial are available. *C. lanceolata* is probably the most reliable, with its various cultivars, though it will suffer some melting out from fungus diseases during periods of high summer heat and humidity. Removing the old faded flower heads is an important part of maintenance of coreopsis. *C. verticillata*, threadleaf coreopsis, doesn't seem as vigorous a plant, but it can be nice with its fine-textured foliage and smaller flowers. For full sun.

Crocosmia (Crocosmia pottsii): Reddish-orange flowers are borne above gladiolus-like foliage in early summer. Grow from small gladiolus-like corms. Spread by underground stems. Excellent cut flower.

Sun to light shade.

Mexican heather (Cuphea hyssopifolia): Tiny purple or white flowers cover this small bushy perennial all summer and until frost in the fall. Height typically reaches 1-2 ft. with a 2-3 ft. spread. Full sun.

Cigar flower (Cuphea micropetala): This is a tough, drought-tolerant perennial that is covered with small yellow and orange, cigar-shaped flowers in the fall. Height typically reaches 3-4 ft. Full sun.

Dianthus spp.: There are several species of dianthus commonly sold. Your success with them as perennials will depend primarily on your planting site. Dianthus needs a well-drained, though not extremely dry, site. One of my new favorites is a tall (18-24 inches) dianthus called 'First Love'. In mixed shades of pink and white, this dianthus has done wonderfully in local trials. The new 'Ideal' cultivars also have done very well. Full sun.

Purple coneflower (Echinacea purpurea): Pinkish-purple flowers with golden brown cone-shaped centers arise on 3-ft. stems from spring until frost. It is one of the easiest and most reliable of perennials to grow in sun to light shade.

Gaura lindheimeri: Small white, pink-tinged flowers arise on long wiry stems above the foliage in the spring and early summer. Prefers a well-drained, sunny site. Very drought-tolerant.

Geranium lancastriense: The leaves of this low-growing geranium look similar to a common weed in the same genus, cranesbill. But the delicate flowers of pale pink, from March to June, will make you glad you didn't mistakenly pull this plant from your garden when you were weeding. Full sun to partial shade.

Swamp sunflower (Helianthus angustifolius): This plant will need pruning constantly until late summer to keep it from getting so tall that it falls over when it blooms in October. Still, it's likely it will reach 5 ft. tall. The flowers are brilliant yellow and very showy. Full sun.

Daylily (Hemerocallis spp.): One of the most versatile and adaptable of perennials, daylilies are available in a myriad of shades and sizes. Most bloom in late spring or early summer. Will tolerate full sun to partial shade and most soil types. Some varieties are evergreen; others die to the ground in winter.

Hosta (Hosta spp.): Hostas, though flowering in

summer, are grown primarily for their large, rich foliage. Strictly for shaded spots, hostas need rich, fertile, moist but well-drained soil.

Louisiana iris (Iris x 'Louisiana'): These are the easiest irises to grow in our area as they are bred from irises native to the South. Available in a tremendous color range. Tolerant of poor drainage. Full sun to partial shade.

Shrimp plant (Justicia brandegeana): Reddish brown flowers resembling shrimp in spring through summer. For sun or partial shade. Reaches several feet in height.

Jacobinia (Justicia carnea): Native to South America, the most popular of this group of plants has terminal clusters of pink flowers on plants up to 2 ft. tall. For sun or shade but prefers filtered sun exposure.

Lantana (Lantana spp.): Vigorous, drought-tolerant, easy-to-grow perennials with aromatic foliage. Very attractive to butterflies. Clusters of flowers, color depending on species. Most are bi- or tri-colored mixtures of yellow, red, pink, white, or orange. Is also a lavender trailing form. For sun or partial shade.

Firespike (Odontonema strictum): May reach 4 ft. tall. Tubular flowers of bright red in early fall are very attractive to hummingbirds. Prefers partial shade.

Firespike Russian sage (Perovskia atriplicifolia): Silvery gray, aromatic foliage with spikes of pale blue flowers borne from late spring through summer. Must be pinched occasionally to prevent it from being so leggy. Prefers sunny, well-drained site.

Blue phlox (Phlox divaricata): Early spring-blooming, low-growing phlox for use in shaded or partially shaded locations. Morning sun and afternoon shade is fine. Needs well-drained soil, but is not drought tolerant. Blooms about the time many spring bulbs bloom.

Border phlox (Phlox paniculata): The common 2-3 ft. tall phlox seen in many gardens. Summer and fall blooming. Primarily in pink, white, and red. For sun or partial shade. Good for the back of the perennial bed or border. All phlox plants seem to get powdery mildew on the leaves, but most seem to tolerate it without spraying.

Phlox stolonifera: Several cultivars of this low-growing, matting phlox exist. 'Miller Crimson' has done well in local trials, with small, showy lavender

flowers from February to May. For full sun.

Moss pink, sometimes called thrift in the South (Phlox subulata): A creeping phlox, only about six inches tall, that is covered with bright pink flowers in early spring for about a month. Mossy, fine textured foliage. Requires good drainage or will rot. Excellent rock garden plant. For sun to light shade.

Plumbago (Plumbago auriculata): In south Florida, plumbago is considered more of a shrub. But in our area, it is killed to the ground by freezes. It begins flowering about June and on through the summer with delicate blue flowers. Grows in full sun or partial shade and is very drought tolerant.

Black-eyed Susan, yellow coneflower, or orange coneflower (Rudbeckia fulgida): Blooms summer to fall with bright yellow flowers having dark centers. Needs full sun and good drainage. Popular cultivar is 'Goldsturm' as it is more compact, up to 2 ft., as opposed to parent which reaches 3 ft. tall.

Mexican petunia (Ruellia brittoniana): Don't plant this one unless you give it loads of room. It will spread, and spread, and spread, by aggressive roots. However, it's very tough and drought-tolerant and has beautiful dark purple flowers all summer and fall. Grows to 3-4 ft. tall. Full sun.

Scarlet sage (Salvia coccinea): Salvia with small, bright red flowers all summer. For full sun or partial shade. May best be treated as an annual except in milder winters.

Pineapple sage (Salvia elegans): Bright red flowers are heaviest in fall. Foliage has a pineapple scent useful for seasoning. Fast-growing, dies to ground in winter but comes back in spring if roots well established and mulched. Easy to root. Sun, light shade.

Blue salvia or blue sage (Salvia farinacea): Widely used perennial salvia available in blue, purple or white-flowering forms. For sun or light shade. 'Victoria' is a blue-purple cultivar. 'Blue Bedder' is more blue. Prune back old flowers to keep the plant blooming its best. Also, may help to prune the whole plant back heavily in late summer. Can tolerate fairly dry conditions.

Autumn sage (Salvia greggii): Native to the arid Southwest, this sage is very drought-tolerant. Doesn't like wet sites. Blooms from spring until hard frost. Doesn't die back in winter. Available in red, pink, white, and salmon colors. Excellent plant for well-drained sites in full sun.

Salvia guaranitica: Medium blue flowers are intermittently produced on this 3-ft. plant from June until frost. Spreads in a rather neat clump. Full sun to light shade.

Salvia x 'Indigo Spires': You must have this perennial in your garden. Long indigo flower spikes are produced from May until frost. Flower color is very intense in the fall. It's a vigorous grower and will require cutting back at least once during the growing season. It reaches 3-4 ft. tall and will become rather leggy unless cut back. Full sun.

Mexican sage (Salvia leucantha): Primarily a fall-blooming salvia with purple-and-white or purple flowers. Becomes rather lanky unless pinched back regularly until mid or late summer. Foliage is gray-green. Very drought-tolerant. Very attractive in fall when in full bloom. For full sun.

Violet sage (Salvia x superba): A compact sage, about one ft. tall, with dark purple flowers. For full sun or partial shade. Blooms heaviest in late spring or early summer.

Sedum 'Autumn Joy': Blooms in late summer to fall with pink or rusty red flowers resembling broccoli florets. Requires full sun and good drainage. Drought tolerant.

Goldenrod (Solidago spp.) : Experts tell us now that goldenrod pollen does not cause hay fever; the culprit is ragweed which blooms inconspicuously at the same time. So, there's no reason not to plant this spectacular fall-blooming plant. English gardeners have used it for years. Several species are available, with plant height dependent on species. For well-drained sites in full sun.

Stoke's aster (Stokesia laevis): Native to the southeast, this early summer blooming perennial is well-adapted to well drained sunny or partially shaded sites. Flowers are blue or white.

Mexican mint marigold or Texas tarragon (Tagetes lucida): Brilliant yellow flowers are produced in the fall. The leaves have the typical tarragon fragrance and flavor and can be used similarly to French tarragon. Full sun.

Verbena canadensis: Heavy flowering pink verbena that spreads rapidly to form a thick mat. For full sun and well-drained sites. Flowers all spring and summer, though flowers heaviest on the newest growth. Drought tolerant. Mite damage is the primary problem.

Verbena tenuisecta: Very drought-tolerant verbena with violet flowers. Commonly seen as a roadside plant as some states' transportation departments have planted it as such. Leaves more finely dissected than *V. canadensis*. Flowers from spring until frost. Mites not as much a problem as with *V. canadensis*. Very tough plant. For sunny, well-drained sites. Will tolerate compacted soils, though.

Veronica spp.: Several veronicas have proven to do well in our area. They are low growing plants which send up blue flower spikes, about a foot tall. The shade of blue and appearance of flower spike varies with species. 'Blue Charm has been especially reliable. 'Goodness Grows' is especially attractive and floriferous, though the heat and humidity of late summer seems to take more of a toll on this particular veronica. For sun.

GROWING ANNUAL FLOWERS

Though perennial flowers have recently made a comeback in popularity, annual flowers will always have their place in the landscape, too. In simple terms, annual flowers are those that live only one growing season.

Winter or fall freezes usually mark the end of warm-season annuals, and summer heat ends the life of cool-season annuals such as pansies. The following year they must be replanted. Some annuals, such as Madagascar periwinkle (vinca) and melampodium do re-seed themselves, though, and come back from seed the following season if the mulch is not too thick.

The primary advantage of annuals over perennials is the speed with which annuals grow and flower. Many annuals will even produce flowers while they are still growing in the cell packs at the nursery. Once in the ground, provided conditions are favorable, they provide quick color for the landscape. And, generally, annuals bloom throughout the season whereas perennials often have a shorter period of bloom. So, even if you favor perennials, you'll still wish to use some annuals to fill in the gaps and take over when the perennials aren't flowering.

STARTING ANNUALS

Most annuals in the landscape are started from small plants you'll purchase from the nursery. Some annuals can be started directly in the ground from seed, but seed establishment directly in the landscape is often not that easy because of moisture fluctuations, eroding rains, and other such environmental factors.

Some gardeners start seed indoors or in a greenhouse, later transplanting the young plants to the landscape. Though you can be quite successful with this technique after a little practice, most people simply don't have the room, patience, or time. So, the vast majority of gardeners just buy young annuals in cell packs from the nursery.

As with perennial flowers, good drainage is important for annual flowers. If you plant them in a soggy, poorly drained soil, chances are they won't live long.

Likewise, if you plant the little plants in a hard, barely cultivated soil, they probably won't fare very well. Take the time to thoroughly work the soil before planting.

Most annuals, as is the case with most perennials, prefer full sun. But, there are some annuals that will tolerate or even prefer moderate to light shade.

Even if you favor perennials, you'll still wish to use some annuals to fill in the gaps and take over when the perennials aren't flowering.

When you plant young annuals, often it is advantageous to pinch the terminal growth to make the plant become bushier. And, as the plant grows during the season, it may require further light pruning of the tips. The summer heat and rains are hard on most annuals. By August, many have become leggy, spindly, and unattractive. A hard late-summer pruning, almost to the ground, will benefit many annuals such as impatiens or begonias. Usually they will come back with new compact growth and still have time to flower before frost.

FERTILIZING, WATERING, AND SLUG CONTROL

Most annuals will benefit from monthly fertilization. Avoid fertilizers with an overly high nitrogen (the first number) ratio to phosphorous and potassium (the second and third numbers). 16-4-8 is okay, however, if half of the nitrogen is water-insoluble or slow-release. Because rates vary with the specific fertilizer ratio used, it's best to follow directions on the bag. 16-4-8 could be used at the rate of 1 cup per 100 sq. ft. for heavy feeders and accordingly less for lighter feeders.

Some annuals don't need monthly fertilization. Annuals such as Madagascar periwinkle (vinca) and portulaca actually prefer less fertile conditions. So, fertilize them less often.

Water often enough to keep your annuals from suffering drought stress, but don't over-water so as to cause root rot. Feel the soil and see when it's dry and learn to note early signs of wilting leaves.

Chewing damage on young flower plants is likely to be from slugs if you don't find insects present. Use a slug paste that you can buy from your garden center. Follow directions and precautions on the label.

ANNUALS THAT MAY SELF-SEED YEAR AFTER YEAR

Alyssum
Bachelor buttons
Calendula
California poppies
Celosia
Cleome
Cosmos
Hollyhocks, including French hollyhock (*Althaea zabrina*)
Impatiens
Larkspur
Melampodium
Nicotiana
Petunias (old fashioned single-flowering type)
Phlox drummondii
Poppies
Portulaca
Sweet alyssum
Verbena
Vinca (Madagascar periwinkle)
Violas (Johnny Jump-ups)
Zinnias

ANNUALS TO PLANT IN THE SPRING
(MARCH-MAY)

Ageratum	Blue or white
Begonias	Pink, red, and white (dark and greenleafed types)
Caladiums	Multi-colored leaves of green, pink, red, and white
Celosia	Red, yellow, pink, orange, and peach
Cleome	Pink and white
Coleus	Multi-colored leaves of red, yellow, or green
Cosmos	Violet, pink, and white
Dianthus (sometimes a perennial)	Pink, red, white, or burgundy
Dusty Miller	Grown for silvery gray foliage
Evolvolus (Blue Daze)	Blue
Foxgloves	White, pink, magenta, yellow
Gomphrena (globe amaranth)	Violet, reddish, and white
Hollyhocks (sometimes a perennial)	Red, pink, and white
Larkspur	Blue, pink, white, violet
Impatiens	Pinks, red, violets, white, orange, and blue
Lobelia	Blue
Marigolds	Various shades of yellow and orange
Melampodium	Yellow
Nicotiana	Red, pink, or white
Pentas	Red, white, pink, and lavender
Petunias	Pink, violet, red, white, blue, salmon
Poppies, Mexican tulip	Yellow
Portulaca	Pink, red, yellow, orange
Salvia	Red, white, salmon, or burgundy
Snapdragons	Red, white, pink, yellow, salmon
Sweet peas	Red, pink, lavender, and white
Torenia	Blues, pinks, white
Verbena	Violet, red, pink, blue, white, salmon
Vinca (Madagascar periwinkle)	Violet, pink, or white
Zinnia	Red, orange, violet, yellow, white, and salmon
Zinnia angustifolia	Orange-yellow, white

ANNUALS TO PLANT IN THE FALL
(OCTOBER-NOVEMBER)

Bachelor buttons	Blue, violet, pink, and white
Calendulas	Yellow-orange
Delphiniums	Blues, whites, and violets
Dianthus (sometimes a perennial)	Pink, red, white, or burgundy
Dusty Miller	Silvery gray foliage
Foxgloves	White, pink, magenta, yellow

Flowering cabbage or kale	Leaves of green and purple or green and white
Hollyhock	Red, white, or pink
Larkspur	Blue, white, pink, violet
Pansies	Blues, purples, orange, white, yellow
Petunias	Pink, violet, red, white, blue, salmon
Poppies, California	Primarily oranges and yellows
Poppies, Iceland	Red, orange, yellow, pink, white
Poppies, Shirley	Red, orange, yellow, pink, white
Snapdragons	Red, white, pink, yellow, salmon
Sweet alyssum	White
Sweet peas	Red, pink, lavender, and white
Violas (Johnny jump-ups)	Purple, white, and yellow

ANNUALS THAT CAN EASILY BE STARTED IN THE MIDST OF SUMMER'S HEAT (JUNE-AUGUST)

Gomphrena (globe amaranth)	Violet, reddish, and white
Impatiens (for shade)	Pinks, red, violets, white, orange, and blue
Marigold	Yellows and oranges
Melampodium	Yellow
Pentas	Red, white, pink, and lavender
Portulaca	Pink, red, yellow, orange
Salvia	Red, white, salmon, or burgundy
Verbena	Violet, red, pink, blue, white, salmon
Vinca	Violet, pink, or white
Zinnia, common	All colors except blue
Zinnia angustifolia	Orange-yellow, white

ANNUALS FOR SUNNY TO ONLY SLIGHTLY SHADED AREAS

Ageratum	Blue or white
Bachelor buttons	Blue, violet, pink, and white
Begonias	Pink, red, and white (dark and green-leafed types)
Flowering cabbage or kale	Leaves of green and purple or green and white
Caladiums	Multi-colored leaves of green, pink, red, and white
Calendulas	Yellow-orange
Celosia	Red, yellow, pink, orange, and peach
Cleome	Pink and white
Cosmos	Violet, pink and white
Delphiniums	Blues, whites and violets
Dianthus (Pinks or Sweet Williams)	Pink, red, white, and burgundy
Dusty Miller	Grown for silvery gray foliage
Evolvolus (Blue Daze)	Blue
Foxglove	White, pink, magenta, yellow
Gomphrena (globe amaranth)	Violet, reddish, and white
Hollyhocks	Red, pink, and white

Impatiens	Pinks, red, violets, white, orange, and blue
Larkspur	Blue, purple, pink, and white
Lobelia	Blue
Marigolds	Various shades of yellow and orange
Melampodium	Yellow
Nicotiana	Red, pink, or white
Pansies	Blues, purples, orange, white, yellow
Pentas	Red, white, pink, and lavender
Petunias	Pink, violet, red, white, blue, salmon
Poppies, California	Primarily oranges and yellows
Poppies, Iceland	Red, orange, yellow, pink, white
Poppies, Mexican tulip	Yellow
Poppies, Shirley	Red, orange, yellow, pink, white
Portulaca	Pink, red, yellow, orange
Salvia	Red, white, salmon, or burgundy
Snapdragons	Red, white, pink, yellow, salmon
Sweet alyssum	White or pink
Sweet peas	Red, pink, lavender, and white
Torenia	Blues, pinks, white
Verbena	Violet, red, pink, blue, white, salmon
Vinca(Madagascar periwinkle)	Violet, pink, or white
Zinnia	Red, orange, violet, yellow, white, and salmon
Zinnia angustifolia	Orange-yellow, white

ANNUALS TOLERANT OF A LITTLE MORE SHADE

most tolerant

Begonias	Pink, red, and white (dark and green-leafed types)
Caladiums *	Multi-colored leaves of green, pink, red, and white
Coleus *	Multi-colored leaves of red, yellow, or green
Evolvolus (Blue Daze)	Blue
Impatiens *	Pinks, red, violets, white, orange, and blue
Melampodium	Yellow
Nicotiana	Red, pink, or white
Pentas	Red, pink, lavender, or white
Salvia	Red, white, salmon, or burgundy
Snapdragon	Red, white, pink, yellow, salmon
Sweet alyssum	White or pink
Torenia	Blues, whites, and pinks

ANNUALS FOR HOT, HARSH, DRY SUNNY AREAS

Gomphrena (globe amaranth)	Violet, reddish, and white
Melampodium	Yellow

Portulaca   Pink, red, yellow, orange
Vinca (Madagascar periwinkle)   Violet, pink, or white
Zinnia angustifolia   Orange-yellow, white

ANNUALS FAIRLY EASY TO SEED DIRECTLY INTO THE LANDSCAPE

Bachelor buttons
Cleome
Cosmos
Gomphrena
Larkspur
Marigold
Nasturtium
Phlox drummondii
Poppies (California, Iceland, and Shirley)
Sweet alyssum
Sweet pea
Sunflower
Zinnia

ANNUALS FOR FRAGRANCE

Nasturtium
Nicotiana
Petunia
Sweet alyssum
Sweet peas

ANNUALS FOR CUT FLOWERS

Bachelor buttons
Calendula
Cleome
Cosmos
Delphinium
Dianthus
Gomphrena
Larkspur
Nasturtium
Poppies
Salvia
Snapdragon
Sunflower
Sweet peas
Verbena
Zinnias

GOOD ANNUALS FOR CONTAINERS

Ageratum
Begonia
Browallia
Coleus
Dianthus
Geranium
Impatiens
Lobelia
Marigold
Nasturtium
Nicotiana
Pansies
Petunias
Phlox
Portulaca
Sweet alyssum
Torenia
Verbena
Vinca (Madagascar periwinkle)

ANNUALS WHICH ATTRACT BIRDS

Bachelor buttons
California poppies
Petunias
Portulaca
Salvia
Sunflower

SPRING-FLOWING BULBS AND OTHER FALL-PLANTED FLOWERS

PLANT SPRING-FLOWING BULBS IN FALL

One way to have color early next spring is to plant spring-flowering bulbs. Planted from November onward through January, the bulbs usually flower sometime during the period from late February into May. Flowering time will depend on time of planting, kind of bulb, and weather.

Daffodils, or other types of narcissus bulbs (of which daffodil is one type), generally perform better in our climatic zone than most other types of spring-flowering bulbs. I've conducted trials with quite a few common cultivars of daffodils in Tallahassee. I've found 'Ice Follies', 'Fortune', 'Gigantic Star', 'Aflame', 'Carlton', 'Trevithian', 'Peeping Tom', and 'Professor Einstein' (in order of performance from best to worst), to be among the most faithful daffodils at coming back year after year once planted. No doubt, though, there are quite a few other cultivars that should be well suited for the Deep South, too.

In my tests, so far I've found no *tulips* that will come back reliably year after year. Given a period of six to eight weeks refrigeration before planting, tulips will usually bloom very well the spring after planting. But don't depend on them blooming in the following years. The foliage will come up in the following springs, but usually few or no flowers emerge. Or, if they do, they're usually not the healthiest looking of flowers.

The problem seems to be our lack of winter chilling. You just have to treat many spring-flowering bulbs as annuals this far south. *Anemones, ranunculuses,* and *hyacinths* fall into the annual category, though hyacinths sometimes will bloom for several springs. Chill hyacinths in the refrigerator before planting. And, soak anemone bulbs in water overnight before planting.

I've had mixed success with *Dutch irises.* Sometimes they've bloomed for years after

> *Planted from November onward through January, the bulbs usually flower sometime during the period from late February into May.*

planting. At other times, one year's bloom was all I got. The same has been true of some of the small bulbs such as scillas. *Snowflakes or snowdrops* (*Leucojum*) are fairly reliable, though.

Despite the one year performance of many bulbs, they're worthy of planting. The flower colors are intense, and in the cool days of early spring, the flowering period is often several weeks to a month. There's no better way to kick off spring.

When planting any of the bulbs, be sure to select a well-drained site. The bulbs will rot in a soil that tends to stay too wet. The planting site also needs to be sunny or only lightly shaded.

The bulbs will perform best if the whole planting bed is tilled before planting. If you simply dig a single hole in the ground and stick in the bulb, root growth may be a struggle. Planting twice the depth of the bulb is a fairly widely accepted rule in our area.

> *When planting any of the bulbs, be sure to select a well-drained site. The bulbs will rot in a soil that tends to stay too wet.*

OTHER FALL-PLANTED FLOWERS

Many *chrysanthemums* can be planted in fall for color. Cut them back after they bloom and they'll flower for you again next fall. You'll need to pinch them back occasionally next spring and summer (until late July) to keep them bushy.

Pansies are the most popular annual planted in fall. They'll provide color through fall, winter, and until the warm days of late spring. The coldest of freezes may nip them back but won't kill them. Plant in full sun and in a well-drained area.

Plant *snapdragons* in fall so they'll be set to bloom early next spring. Petunias planted in fall will bloom then, and provided winter freezes aren't too severe, into late next spring. Both snaps and petunias, as most all flowers, like full sun and well-drained soils.

Delphiniums will flower in the spring if planted in fall. Some local nurseries have plants, or you may have to order plants. Don't depend on the delphiniums surviving the summer heat and perennializing this far south, though. They may, but more likely the delphiniums will just be a spectacular annual for you with their spikes of brilliant blue flowers.

Some *flower seeds* need to be planted in fall if the flowers are to be at the blooming stage next spring. *Bachelor buttons, sweet peas, various poppies,* and *alyssum* are examples. All are relatively easy to start, provided (you guessed it!) you pick a sunny, well-drained site.

Flowers planted in fall will require light monthly applications of fertilizer through the winter. They will also require pinching to make them branch and keep them from having long, lanky stems. Water them as needed.

Cold will not be a big concern with most of the flowers. They're classified as hardy annuals, meaning they can handle normal freezes. Petunias, however, won't tolerate too many hours of temperature too far below freezing. Unless we have a mild winter, they'll likely require some protection some nights. Covering with a light cloth or a light layer of pine straw may be all that is needed. They won't survive a hard freeze without more protection, though.

There are many flowering perennials that will give you color early next spring if planted in fall. Fall is a prime time for planting flowering perennials because the plants have all winter to get their roots established and put on some top growth. Come spring, the plants are often ready to flower. They will be much further ahead of plants which you wait until spring to plant. The same principle applies to perennial shrubs such as azaleas. Fall is a much better planting time than spring. Spring is a time to enjoy the fruits of your fall planting.

10

Growing Fruit at Home

for Food and Beauty

THE REWARDS AND THE PROBLEMS

Growing fruit in the home landscape can be rewarding. One reward is, of course, the fresh fruit. There's just no comparison between peaches you buy in the grocery store and peaches you grow yourself.

There is an additional reward in the attractiveness of many of the fruit plants. Consider, for example, the pink flowers of a peach tree in spring or the orange fruit of a persimmon tree against a blue autumn sky.

But growing fruit at home can have its problems, too. Insect pests and fungus diseases like fresh fruit as much as people do. You'll have to protect your fruit from such pests if you are to be successful. Use one of the fruit tree sprays (combination insecticide/fungicide) available from garden centers. Follow label instructions carefully.

DIFFICULT-TO-GROW FRUIT

Don't lump all fruit into the difficult-to-grow category, though. Some types of fruit can be grown without a lot of spraying. First, let's quickly look at the fruit you may wish to avoid unless you have the time and discipline to stay on a regular preventative spray schedule.

Peaches are a good example. Unless you routinely spray peaches from the flower bud stage up until harvest, you'll find it extremely difficult to avoid a host of pests. Chances are you'll end up with wormy fruit if any fruit.

Nectarines and *plums* fall into the same category as peaches. *Apples*, though not as troubled by pests as peaches, nectarines, and plums, sometimes tend to have their share of pests, too. So do *bunch grapes*. Muscadine grapes usually have fewer problems.

Pecans are among the most difficult of the fruit and nut trees to grow, especially if you select the wrong pecan variety. Plant a pecan for shade and be thankful for any nuts you may get in the home landscape situation.

Pecans fall prey to a number of problems, pecan scab disease being one of the most serious. Commercial pecan producers spray six or seven times a season with special pecan sprayers designed to reach the tops of the trees. Even with the proper spraying, production is sometimes limited due to the alternate year bearing habit of the pecan.

If you plant pecan trees at home, plant one of the varieties that has some degree of resistance to scab disease. Elliott, Curtis, Stuart, Desirable, and Moreland are the recommended varieties for plantings that will not be sprayed. Fertilize the pecan trees each February (50 lbs. of fertilizer for mature trees) and hope for the best. Pecan weevils, aphids, and rainy springs still can limit production, but spraying in the home garden is not feasible.

EASIER-TO-GROW FRUIT

Pears, figs, blueberries, blackberries, and

muscadine grapes can be among the easiest of fruits to grow at home. But, with all of these, there are certain factors to consider. None are completely fool-proof.

The *pear's* biggest enemy is fire blight disease. Varieties recommended for the Deep South are generally fire blight resistant. Avoid varieties such as Bartlett that aren't resistant. If you further minimize possibility of fire blight problems by not over-fertilizing and pruning lightly on an annual basis, you will probably have few problems growing pears.

Figs have been grown in home landscapes for years without any spraying. The fig's number one enemy is the nematode, a microscopic worm that feeds on its root system. But, by mulching the plant well and occasionally fertilizing, you can usually help the plant tolerate nematodes. There is no chemical treatment for nematodes anyway.

Rabbiteye blueberries are very picky about soil requirements. It's necessary that they have an acidic soil of pH not higher than about 5.2. But, provide the blueberries with their acidic soil and interplant them with the proper pollinator variety, and they'll usually have few problems. Beware; you can kill young plants by over-fertilizing.

*B*e sure to plant in a spot that receives full sun all day. Otherwise, fruit production will be poor.

To provide an acidic soil, don't plant blueberries within 20 feet of a house. Lime from the house foundation decreases soil acidity. Mix from ¼ to ½ cubic foot of Canadian peatmoss with the planting soil. Keep the plants heavily mulched with pine straw, pine bark, or oak leaves. Don't use grass clipping as mulch.

Blackberries sometimes have a problem with fungus diseases. But, generally, if you'll do a thorough job of removing old canes immediately after harvest, you'll have less of a problem.

Muscadine grapes can have pest problems from time to time. But, you don't have to keep the on a preventative spray schedule in the home garden situation. The most important factor to remember when growing muscadine grapes is to prune heavily each year (remove everything but short spurs with 2-3 buds each on the two or four main arms). And be sure to interplant the proper pollinator variety.

Other types of fruit that don't have to be on a preventative spray program (but that may have to be sprayed occasionally) are *persimmons, satsumas,* and *kumquats.* Even apples may be grown sometimes without preventative sprays. But, peaches, nectarines, plums, and bunch grapes generally require sprays to prevent pest problems from overcoming them.

One final and very important word of advice on growing fruit: Be sure to plant in a spot that receives full sun all day. Otherwise, fruit production will be poor.

PICKING THE RIGHT DECIDUOUS FRUIT VARIETIES FOR OUR AREA

Remember that we still don't have as much cold here as our friends further north. So we can't grow all the same kinds of fruit trees that they can grow.

Many types of fruit trees have a requirement for winter chilling. Unless that chilling requirement is met, the plant will not fruit well and will usually gradually die. So, despite the temptations of the mail-order catalogue pictures and the bargain prices in some of the discount stores, stick to fruit varieties known to perform well in your specific area. There will even be slight differences between what can be grown in Macon, Georgia and Tallahassee, Florida, though Macon is less than 200 miles north of Tallahassee.

Avoid fruits such as cherries that just don't grow here in the Deep South. And, though you may have fond memories of the taste of a particular apple or peach from your childhood in the north, don't try to grow it here.

The chart below, compiled by Dr. Tim Crocker of the University of Florida, lists many of the fruit varieties that will grow in the lower part of zone 8. If you're in the northern half of zone 8, you will need to visit or phone your local county extension service office for a list of local variety recommendations. Though you should do fine with the varieties on this list, new varieties are constantly becoming available.

*M*any types of fruit trees have a requirement for winter chilling. UNless that chilling requirement is met, the plant will not fruit well and will usually gradually die.

APPLES
Anna
Dorsett Golden
 (as pollinator
 for Anna)

BLUEBERRIES For pollination, interplant...
(Aliceblue, Beckyblue, Climax, Bonita)...
(Bluegem, Woodard)...(Brightwell, Delite,
Tifblue, Choice, Briteblue, Southland)

CHESTNUTS
Chinese type
AU-Cropper
AU-Leader
AU-Homestead
Black Beauty
**Chinese-
American hybrids**
Blue Ridge
Lucky 13
Carpenter

RASPBERRIES
Dorman Red

PERSIMMONS
Non-astringent:
Fuyugaki
Hanafuyu
O'Gosho
Astringent:
Hachiya
Saijo
Tamopan
Tanenashi
Gailey (is required pollinator for Hachiya)

PLUMS
Excelsior
Mariposa
Early Bruce
Methley
Ozark Premier
Kelsey
(all require cross-pollination except Methley)

FIGS
Brown Turkey
Celeste
Green Ischia
Alma
Magnolia

BLACKBERRIES
Brazos
Cheyenne
Comanche
Cherokee

Plant
Flordagrand &
Oklawaha
together for
pollination.

NECTARINES
Armking
Sunfre
Sunrich
Sungold
Sunlite

PEACHES
Springcrest
Springbrite
June Gold
Flordaking
Maygold
Rio Grande
Suwannee
Sunhigh

PEARS
Softest:
Flordahome
Baldwin
Hood
Others:
Pineapple
Tenn
Ayres
Orient
Carnes

For pollination,
plant Hood with
Pineapple or
Flordahome

BUNCH GRAPES
Lake Emerald
Blue Lake
Stover
Conquistador
Daytona
Suwannee

PECANS
**(Disease-
resistant)**
Stuart
Elliott
Curtis
Desirable
Moreland

MUSCADINE GRAPES
Southland
Magoon
Higgins
Dixie
Regale
Fry
Jumbo
Carlos
Welder
Cowart
Chief
Noble
Nesbitt
Summit
Granny Val
(Fry, Jumbo,
Higgins, and
Summitt
are female and
require
interplanting
 with one of the
other cultivars)

COLD-HARDY CITRUS FRUITS

Several kinds of citrus fruits can be grown in the warmer parts of the Deep South despite our cold spells during the winter. Satsuma, a citrus fruit very similar to a tangerine, and kumquat, a small citrus fruit which may be eaten peel and all, are the two most commonly grown cold-hardy citrus in our area.

The duration of freezing temperatures is more of a factor in causing freeze damage to citrus than is the actual temperature. For example, a brief drop to 24 degrees may cause no harm. But, several hours at 26 degrees may cause damage, particularly if the plant has had no previous exposure to freezing temperatures that season. As the days shorten and nights become cooler, plants slow top growth and attain a degree of winter hardiness. Satsumas might tolerate 15 degrees in January when they are completely dormant. But a temperature of 26 degrees might cause serious damage in mid-November.

So, regardless what type of citrus you plant in the lower South, there is always the possibility of cold damage. But, by selecting the most cold-hardy types, you greatly decrease the probability of damage.

Kumquats are undoubtedly the most cold tolerant of the commonly available citrus, tolerating temperatures down to 10 degrees when fully dormant. Active growth occurs only at relatively high temperatures, so the plants remain semi-dormant during late fall, winter, and early spring. They bloom later than other citrus and cease active growth earlier in the fall. So, they are better able to tolerate the winter's cold.

Kumquat trees rarely reach ten feet tall. As with all citrus in our area, kumquat trees are normally grown on trifoliate orange rootstock to impart cold hardiness. The trifoliate root stock further reduces the kumquat's natural height.

The kumquat fruit, produced in large numbers, are yellow to bright orange, and are generally no larger than 1¾ inches in diameter.

The fruit matures in the fall and holds well on the tree without much loss of quality. They may be eaten fresh, peel included, or may be preserved as marmalade or candied whole fruit.

'Nagami', 'Meiwa', and 'Marumi' are the three common kumquat varieties. 'Nagami' is more acidic than the others. 'Meiwa', which produces nearly round, sweet fruit, has become very popular for landscape use.

Satsumas are very similar to the tangerines you buy at the grocery store. Mature, dormant satsuma trees have survived 15 degree freezes without serious injury. Satsuma trees are medium to small in size. It's usually best to plant them in a sunny spot on the south side of the house where they will be shielded from north winds. Planted in such a spot, the northern winds often limit the tree's height to the height of the house.

Satuma fruit matures in October to November but doesn't hold quality on the tree much longer than two weeks. They become puffy and lose flavor and juice content if left on the tree too long. Fruits become fully ripened for eating while the peel is still rather green. Not all fruit ripens at the same time.

'Meyer' lemon, though, one of the most cold-hardy lemon selections, is only cold-hardy into the mid 20's. The fruit ripening period usually lasts for several months beginning in late summer. Good crops of large, practically seedless, juicy lemons are produced.

With care, and cooperation from Old Man Winter, *grapefruits* can be grown in the lower areas of zone 8. 'Duncan', an early-ripening, white-fleshed variety is available from some nurseries. However, grapefruit plants may be killed to the ground in really hard freezes. If you grow grapefruit, you need to have some method of protecting the plant during the freezes. A plastic-covered frame, supplemented with a light bulb, might work during mild freezes. A wire cage, wrapped around the tree and stuffed with pine needles or hay to insulate the trunk, may be necessary during severe freezes.

Try to always plant citrus on the south or southwestern side of the house in a sunny spot. Such an exposure, especially if close to the house, will provide the little bit of extra protection from the northern winds that can make the difference between life and death.

PRUNING TREES TO THE PROPER SHAPE STARTS AT PLANTING TIME

As soon as fruit trees are planted, they need to be pruned to begin training them to the proper shape. To severely prune a tree you may have just paid $10-$15 for is an emotional task. But, it must be done if the tree is to grow to the desired form.

From then on, pruning needs to be done every

year. It's generally done in January and early February.

Fruit trees are pruned for several reasons. It's desirable to keep the trees at a height that will facilitate easy harvesting. Pruning also removes excess leaf growth that will shade fruit and inhibit ripening. Probably most importantly, though, pruning creates and maintains a strong structure to bear and hold the fruit crop.

Pruning should always remove branches that interfere with the basic framework of the tree or branches that run against each other. Try to select limbs that have a wide angle of attachment rather than a narrow angle which may split as the limbs grow larger, pushing against each other, and loading down with fruit.

Apple and pear trees, when purchased, are often unbranched sticks about 4 ft. tall. They should be cut back to about 3 ft. so that they will branch below that point the first growing season. Next winter when you prune, retain the central trunk and three or four spirally arranged branches around the trunk. The lowest branch should be at least 2 ft. above ground.

The second winter after planting, the central stems or trunks of apple or pear trees need to be cut back to balance them with the other branches. You do not want any one branch to develop significant growth and height dominance over the others.

Mature apple and pear trees should not be heavily topped each year. Moderate annual pruning to remove dense inner growth, crossover branches, and some length is preferable to heavy pruning every three or four years. Heavy pruning upsets the balance of the tree, causing a proliferation of water sprouts.

Peach trees need to be cut back to about knee high at planting time. Leave several spirally arranged branches on the trunk. Reduce the length of the side branches so that only several buds remain on each branch. Remove all lower branches. The objective is to develop three or four primary framework branches and no central trunk.

Plum trees are pruned much the same as peach trees, but you may leave more than just three or four framework branches on a plum tree.

During the second winter after planting the peach, cut back each of the three or four selected framework branches to about $^2/_3$ their length. The objective is to cause each of the framework limbs to branch into two more branches. This will increase the number of framework branches from three or four to six or eight.

Plum trees tend to develop somewhat of an open center naturally without the hard pruning required on a peach.

Prune peach and plum trees every year. Remove any crossing branches and those that are growing into the center. Then shorten the tree considerably by cutting back limbs to outwardly facing buds.

Pecan or persimmon trees need to have the upper $^1/_3$ of the young tree's main trunk removed at planting time.

In the second winter, remove all limbs within four feet of the ground from the trunk of the pecan tree. Remove persimmon branches closer than two feet to the ground. If two limbs form a narrow angle of attachment, remove one of them. Otherwise, they will push against each other as they grow and may eventually split.

Mature pecan and persimmon trees require little pruning. Hopefully, you trained the trees in early years so that branches come off the trunk at wide angles rather than narrow angles.

Cut back *fig* plants to about half their height when planting.

The second winter after planting the fig, thin out dense growth and eliminate dead wood. Retain three to eight strong, upright sprouts at least 3-4 inches apart at the base.

Figs will need occasional shortening of the main branches to keep the bushes to a manageable height. Thin out weak growth and remove dead wood.

Young *grape* vines are cut back at planting time to a point on the most vigorous cane so that only two buds are left. All other canes are removed.

The grape cane you selected at planting time should reach the top wire of the trellis during the first growing season. If not, you'll have to select another cane and try again the second year. If, however, the selected cane does reach the top wire, cut it at that point the following winter so that a lateral will branch out each way along the trellis wire. Be sure to leave at least one lateral shoot to grow each way on the bottom trellis wire, too.

When pruning in later year, remove all *bunch grape* canes or arms except for one cane on each wire. Leave short spurs with two or three buds on the main trunk when removing the old canes. The buds on these spurs will form next year's fruiting arms and will be the arms retained at next year's pruning.

The main arms on *muscadine grape* vines are never removed. But all small or twiggy growth on these arms is cut back to a point leaving only two or three buds per growth spur. Don't worry about sap that may bleed from the cuts; it's mostly just water.

Blueberry plants do not have to be pruned severely at planting time. But they should not be allowed to fruit the first season after planting. At planting time, prune or pick off the fruiting buds at the ends of the shoots.

The main objective in pruning blueberries is the promotion of strong new wood. If too little pruning is done, the plants are crowded with twiggy weak growth. Either remove or cut back old canes that have little strong new wood. Eliminate the twiggy growth in the top and outer areas of the bushes.

Blackberries and *raspberries* are pruned just after harvest by removing all old canes.

PRUNING OVERGROWN AND NEGLECTED FRUIT TREES

Most of us wouldn't make very good commercial fruit growers. Mostly out of fear of making a mistake, we're overly hesitant to prune our fruit trees. Yet, well thought out pruning can help a tree to bear more and better fruit.

If you're like most home gardeners, chances are you have a fruit tree or two that has hardly been pruned since it was planted. Now it's so thick and overgrown you just don't know where to start.

Probably you should begin by removing branches that cross over each other or that rub. Basically, you want to remove most larger growth headed back toward the center of the tree. You should try to select the outwardly headed limbs to keep. If there's too much growth inside the tree, it will prohibit light from reaching the interior of the tree and will, therefore, reduce fruit production and ripening.

Some trees, such as pears, and to a lesser degree, apples, naturally grow upward. You'll not have to do as much thinning on these trees as with a peach or nectarine tree. But, some thinning will be required.

If large limbs are allowed to grow toward the inside of the tree, soon they'll cross other branches. Soon those crossing branches become rubbing branches, causing injury to the branches they rub against. So, your first step is to thin the tree, removing such inwardly growing branches.

When thinning the tree, remove entire limbs. Don't merely shorten limbs. Cut the limb off back at the trunk or at the main limb from which it starts.

Contrary to what you may have heard for years, there's no need to paint the wound with pruning paint. Just make a good, clean cut. Don't leave a stub. But, don't cut so close, either, that you remove the little ridge of bark that connects the branch being removed with the trunk or main limb to which it is attached. That small ridge, called the branch ridge collar, contains the cells from which callus tissue will begin growing over the wound. If you injure the collar, healing will not be complete.

Next, look at the outwardly growing branches. If two branches interfere with each other, you'll have to make a decision as to which branch to remove. They can't both stay. Keep the stronger, better placed limb.

After you've removed all the crossing and rubbing branches on the tree, then you still may need to do more thinning. Remove dead or diseased branches. After doing so, sterilize your pruning tools with alcohol before cutting into healthy wood. Otherwise, you may spread the disease organism.

After removing dead or diseased branches, remove spindly growth and water sprouts. Such growth usually has no or few flowers and so will produce no fruit.

After you've thinned the tree so that more light can enter and so that branches aren't interfering with each other, you can consider reducing the size of the tree. Be careful, though. If you've let your tree grow unchecked for years, a drastic size reduction now may stimulate excessive vegetative growth at the expense of fruit production next season. Also, the succulent growth stimulated may be more susceptible to disease organisms, such as fire blight disease on pears and apples.

To reduce the size of the tree, you'll shorten limbs. When you shorten a limb, you destroy the dominance that limb's tip once had and establish the limbs just below the pruning cut as the new dominant growing points. So, when making your shortening cuts, cut back to outward growing limbs. If you cut back to an inward growing limb, it will become the new dominant growing point. But, because it's growing inward, you'll end up having to remove it later when it becomes a crossing or rubbing branch.

In a nutshell, that's all there is to pruning overgrown fruit trees. Of course, it's best not to let your trees become overgrown in the first place. Start pruning at the time you plant the young trees, training them to the proper shape. Then, each winter, make the necessary corrections and size reductions, keeping in mind that some trees will require more severe pruning than others.

FERTILIZING FRUIT TREES

Fruit trees generally need some fertilizer to obtain the nutrients necessary for plant growth. But, over-fertilization can result in vigorous growth that interferes with good fruit production.

There is no one particular fertilizer that has to be used. The general purpose fertilizers such as 10-10-10 are usually adequate.

When fertilizing, spread the fertilizer on the ground under the tree branches and slightly beyond. Water it in if possible. Never merely heap the fertilizer in one or two piles.

SPECIAL NOTE ON FERTILIZATION RECOMMENDATIONS

As mentioned in the following section on fertilization, some trees are very susceptible to over-fertilization. The fertilization recommendations given can be varied, and often need to be varied in accordance with the growth rate of your plants. But, always tend to vary in the direction of using less rather than more fertilizer.

Peaches, nectarines, and plums: The March after the trees have been planted, apply 1 cup of 10-10-10 spread over an area 3 ft. in diameter. Each February thereafter, apply about 1½ cups of 10-10-10 fertilizer for each year of age of the tree until a maximum of 10-15 cups is reached as the tree ages.

Apples: Fertilize the same as for peaches and plums. If you severely prune the apple tree, don't apply any fertilizer that year. Similarly, if growth is excessive, stop fertilizing for a year or two until growth slows to a more normal rate (10-15 inches per year of terminal growth).

Pecans and Chinese chestnuts: Apply 1½ cups of 10-10-10 fertilizer per tree the first season after planting in May. In succeeding years, apply 2-3 cups of fertilizer per year of age of a pecan tree in February. The maximum rate for mature pecans is 50 lbs. Chestnuts require about 1 cup for each year of age up to a maximum of 15 lbs. Pecans may also require zinc. If the fertilizer you use doesn't contain one unit of zinc, apply zinc as zinc oxide or zinc sulfate. On older trees, zinc oxide may be applied at the rate of 1⅓ cups per tree each year. Zinc sulfate may be applied at the rate of 5⅓ cups per tree on mature trees. Zinc sulfate applications last 2-3 years.

Grapes: Before spring growth begins the first year grapes are planted, apply ¼ cup of 10-10-10 around each plant. Spread the fertilizer, keeping it at least 6 inches from the vine. Repeat at monthly intervals until July. On 2-year plants, use ½ cup at each monthly application. Bearing vines will need 2½ cups of fertilizer per plant, applied in late February.

Blueberries: Never over-fertilize young blueberries; you can easily kill them! After new growth begins the first year, apply 2 ounces of acid azalea-camellia fertilizer (4-8-8), or ¾ ounce if the formulation is 12-4-8 or similar. In June, apply 1 ounce of ammonium sulfate per plant or 2 ounces of the 4-8-8 azalea-camellia fertilizer, or ¾ ounce of the 12-4-8 azalea-camellia fertilizer. Don't apply the fertilizer within 6 inches of the trunk.

In late February of the second growing season, apply 3 ounces of the 4-8-8 azalea-camellia special or 1 ounce of the 12-4-8 azalea-camellia special. In June, apply 2 oz. of ammonium sulfate, 3 oz. of 4-8-8, or 1 oz. of 12-4-8 per plant.

For the third season and later, use a fertilizer, such as the 12-4-8 azalea-camellia special, high in nitrogen and low in phosphorous. In late February of the third growing season, apply 3 oz. per plant. After harvest, apply another 3 oz., being sure to keep the fertilizer away from the trunk.

Fertilization in future years should be done twice a year in late February and immediately after harvest. Increase the amount of 12-4-8 applied by one ounce per year of plant age, not to exceed 6 oz. for the spring application on large plants. The post-harvest application should not exceed 5 oz. per plant.

Blackberries: About a month after planting, sprinkle ⅓ cup of 10-10-10 in a 24-inch circle around each plant. In June, sprinkle ⅓ cup of fertilizer over a 30-inch circle.

Mature blackberry vines should receive three applications of ⅓-½ cup of 10-10-10 per year. Make the first application in February, another shortly after harvest, and a third in late August.

Pears: Apply one cup of 10-10-10 per tree per year of age up to a maximum of 12 cups. Apply half of this amount in late February before growth begins and the other half after the fruit is set. Spread the fertilizer over the area beneath the branch spread of the tree and slightly beyond. If you don't get fruit set, omit the second application.

If the trees are heavily pruned, reduce the amount of fertilization for a year or two. Also, if shoot growth on trees exceeds 6 inches annually, reduce the rate of fertilization. Too much vegetative growth on pears can lead to fire blight disease.

Figs: In moderately fertile soils, figs may grow satisfactorily without fertilizer. But, in infertile, sandy soils, or where competition from other plants is heavy, fertilizer is needed.

For fertilizing 1-2 yr. old plants, apply ⅓ cup of 10-10-10 each month from March through the end of July. On older plants, apply fertilizer three times a year: late February, early June, and mid-July. Use ⅓ cup of fertilizer per foot of plant height at each application. If the fruit are not reaching maturity and ripening properly, excess fertilizer or drought may be the problem and fertilization should be reduced. Always keep a fig bush well mulched, preferably mulched all the way out to the tips of the branches. Spread your fertilizer over this mulch and water it in.

Persimmons: If your persimmon tree is in a lawn area, it will receive adequate fertilizer from that supplied to the lawn. Excess nitrogen will result in fruit drop. Trees are very likely to drop their fruit anyway during the early years of their life. Also, a heavy crop one year may result in a light crop the following year. To reduce this problem, thin the fruit to 6 inches apart on oriental persimmons within a month after bloom if a heavy crop is formed.

PEST CONTROL

As mentioned already at the beginning of this chapter under the section, "The Rewards and the Problems", fruit trees certainly have their share of pests. Some of these pest problems can be reduced by careful cultural management of the plants. But some will require preventative pesticide sprays.

If you have just a few fruit trees, the easiest way for you to approach pest control is to purchase what is normally referred to at garden centers as a "fruit tree spray" or "home orchard spray". Such pesticides are a combination of fungicide and insecticide formulated for use on home fruit trees. Buy one that has complete directions for the type of fruit you have. And spray religiously according to the directions.

For many fruits, you will need to start spraying before the flowers even open in the spring. The pesticide label should give you the correct timing for sprays. The key, though, is to start on a spray program early, before the growing season starts and well before the pest problem develops. Unfortunately, you must prevent most pest problems. You don't have the option of curing them once they develop.

If rigidly followed spray programs using the pre-formulated home orchard sprays don't work, contact your local county extension office for further recommendations.

WEED CONTROL

Practically all fruit trees need full sun in order to produce fruit. In planting, avoid shaded spots and areas where root competition from other plants is heavy. Keep grass away from the base of the tree or vine. Grass competition takes a heavy toll. Some plants, such as figs and blueberries need to be mulched. Use pine bark, pine straw, cypress mulch, leaves, or other organic material. Maintain a 2-3 inch thick mulch extending out to the branch tips.

Just as around landscape plants, Glyphosate herbicides (such as Roundup® and other brands) can be used around many fruit trees as directed sprays to kill emerged weeds. Refer to the herbicide label for specific recommendations and plant clearances. But, avoid getting any of the herbicide spray mixture on trunks of plants such as blueberries or young peaches, nectarines, or plums. The green tissue in such trunks will absorb the glyphosate, and damage or death of the plant can result. Always, follow the directions and precautions on the pesticide label carefully! They can save you much grief!

12
Vegetables

For Freshness and Enjoyment

Growing vegetables in the home landscape is a popular hobby for several reasons. First, it can be profitable. The garden produce can save money in the family budget. Also, some vegetables, such as tomatoes have to be picked before they are fully ripe if they are to be sold in the grocery store. Home-grown tomatoes, on the other hand, can be left on the plant until they are ripe. Home-grown tomatoes are, indeed, tastier.

Finally, there is the enjoyment or therapy that comes from planting seed and nurturing it to maturity. Some people like to unwind at the end of a hard day by working in their rose garden; others prefer the sanctity of their vegetable garden.

You don't necessarily have to have a "vegetable garden", though, to grow vegetables. You can grow a few tomatoes, squash, cucumbers, peppers, or other such vegetables in small areas of your home landscape, maybe even tucked away in shrub or flower beds. Plants that are relatively compact and produce a lot of vegetables on one plant lend themselves well to such an arrangement. But, don't try to grow sweet corn, beans, or peas on a few plants mixed in with your shrubs and flowers.

Vegetable gardening is pretty much a year-round thing in the Deep South.

You'll never accumulate enough harvest at one time to make a meal.

Tomatoes, especially, can provide large harvests in small spaces. If you grow tomatoes in a raised bed of compost-like material, using lots of organic matter and fertilizer along with the soil, you can produce tremendous numbers of fruit.

THE SEASONS OF VEGETABLE GARDENING IN THE DEEP SOUTH

Vegetable gardening is pretty much a year-round thing in the Deep South. The mid and late summer, because of the heat, will be the slowest season. Insects and diseases will be at their peak then, too, so many gardeners concentrate more on spring, fall, and winter gardens.

Spring garden: The spring garden is by far the most popular. It's really what is considered a summer garden a little further north.

Determining exactly when to plant the spring garden usually involves a little bit of gambling. You want to plant many of the seeds and plants as soon as possible after frost. The sooner you plant, the sooner you can harvest vegetables before the insects and diseases overwhelm the plants in the summer. But, if you plant too early, a late spring freeze may kill some of the tender plants such as tomatoes. Mid to late March is normally the time to plant most of the plants for the spring garden. Some plants, being cool-season

*T*he sooner you plant, the sooner you can harvest vegetables before the insects and diseases overwhelm the plants in the summer.

plants, need to be planted even earlier than March, though.

Here's a list of *warm-season vegetables* for the spring garden and when they can be planted. You'll note that some of the vegetables can be planted on through the summer, whereas others shouldn't be planted after March or April until possibly again in late summer or early fall for the fall garden.

Snap beans: March-April
Pole beans March-April
Lima beans: March-August
Cantaloupes: March-April
Sweet corn: March-April
Cucumbers: March-April
Eggplant: March-July
Okra: April-July
Southern peas: March-August
Peppers: March-April
Sweet potatoes: March-June
Pumpkins: March-April
Summer squash: March-April
Winter squash: March
Tomatoes: March-April
Watermelons: March-April

Some cool-season vegetables can also be planted in the early spring vegetable garden. Here's a list and the timing for planting. Note that most of these can also be grown in the winter garden, planted in the fall. February or March is generally the latest you can plant most of these.

Beets: September-March
Broccoli: August-February
Cabbage: September-February
Carrots: September-March
Cauliflower: January-February
Celery: January-March
Chinese cabbage: October-January
Collards February-March
Endive/escarole: February-March
Kohlrabi: March-April

Lettuce: February-March
Mustard: January-March
Bunching onions: August-March
Parsley: February-March
English peas: January-March
Irish potatoes: January-March
Radishes: September-March
Turnips: January-April

Summer garden: A few of the warm-season vegetables will stand the summer heat. Still, insects and diseases will be a major problem during the summer. So, most likely you'll have to do some spraying. Here are the vegetables that you can plant for a summer garden and the dates they can be planted. Note that they're only part of the spring garden list:

Lima beans: March-August
Eggplant: March-July
Okra: March-July
Southern peas: March-August
Peppers: July-August
Sweet potatoes: March-June
Watermelons: July-August

Fall warm-season garden: In the late days of summer, you can begin planting your fall garden. The night temperatures begin to moderate a bit, so the plants will grow a little better again. And, there's still time to produce a warm-season crop before frost. Still, insect populations will be high. So, expect more trouble than with your spring garden. Here are some warm-season crops that could be included:

Snap beans: August-September
Pole beans: August-September
Lima beans: August
Sweet corn: August
Cucumbers: August-September
Southern peas: August
Peppers: August
Pumpkin: August
Summer squash: August-September
Tomatoes: August
Watermelons: August

Fall and Winter Cool-season garden: As nights begin cooling down a little in September, you can begin planting many of the cool-season vegetables again.

Beets: September-March
Broccoli: August-February
Cabbage: September-February
Carrots: September-March
Cauliflower: August-October and Jan.-Feb.
Chinese cabbage: October-January
Collards: August-November
Endive/escarole: September
Kohlrabi: October-November
Lettuce: September
Mustard: September-May
Bulbing onions: September-December
Radishes: September-March
Spinach: October-November
Strawberries: September-October
Turnips: August-October

CONSIDERATIONS IN WHERE TO PLANT VEGETABLES

Where you plant your vegetables has a lot to do with how successful you'll be at producing a plentiful harvest.

Sunlight: Most vegetables need full sun all day long. Some of the leafy crops such as collards, spinach, or broccoli can tolerate partial shade, but not complete shade.

Tree root competition: Don't plant near trees or large hedges. The vegetables will do poorly because of competition for moisture and nutrients.

Good drainage: Don't plant in a poorly drained area. The times you can cultivate the garden will be limited. And, root rots, stem rots, and other soil-borne diseases will likely be a problem.

Most vegetables need full sun all day long.

Water supply: Vegetables need good drainage, but they also need water. You may produce a crop some years without any irrigation. But, most years there are dry periods when the ability to irrigate will be vital to the success of the garden.

SOIL PREPARATION

SOIL TESTS AND LIMING

Several months before you intend to plant your vegetable garden, contact your local county extension service office for materials to send a soil sample to your state university soil testing lab. The lab test will tell you if you need to apply lime to the soil to raise the pH to a level more favorable for vegetables. If you find that you do, proceed with soil preparation, as given below, and mix in the required amount of lime to a depth of 6-8 inches. Do not lime unless a reliable soil test, such as the state lab test, indicates the need. You could apply too much lime.

If you don't get around to checking your soil pH well in advance of planting, you can still apply lime up to one or two weeks before planting. However, the lime will not fully lower the pH to the desired point until your vegetables are much further along. So, if possible, plan well ahead to check your soil pH and add lime if needed.

CULTIVATION AND INCORPORATION OF ORGANIC MATTER

Vegetable plants need a thoroughly worked soil. You can cultivate small areas with a shovel and hoe, but for areas of much size, you'll need a rototiller. You may consider renting one for the garden preparation if you don't own one or can't borrow one.

Cultivate the soil as deeply as you can at least three weeks before planting time. It's impossible to cultivate too deeply. The addition of organic soil amendments isn't absolutely necessary, but is certainly can help. Mix in organic matter well in advance of planting, preferably at least a month before seeding, unless it is well-composted. Well-composted materials can be

Animal manures, rotted leaves, compost, or cover crops all make good soil amendments. Mix them into the existing soil; don't merely spread them over the surface.

applied at planting time. Animal manures, rotted leaves, compost, or cover crops all make good soil amendments. Mix them into the existing soil; don't merely spread them over the surface. Crimson clover, rye, or vetch are possible winter cover crops that can be tilled into the soil when preparing the spring garden.

FERTILIZING BEFORE PLANTING

Unless you use large quantities of organic matter and a variety of organic matter, you will need to use some commercial fertilizer in your vegetable garden. Grades such as 8-8-8, 10-10-10, or 20-20-20 give good results with most vegetable crops. If the soil pH is above 6.3, select a fertilizer that contains micro-nutrients.

A week or so before planting, spread (broadcast) the fertilizer over the entire vegetable garden at the rate of 2-4 lbs. of 8-8-8 or 10-10-10 per 100 sq. ft. If you use 15-15-15 or 20-20-20, use only 1-2 lbs. per 10 sq. ft.

At planting time, band 1-2 lbs. of fertilizer per 100 ft. of row in one or two bands each two to three inches to the side and one to two inches below the seed level or plant row.

One pint of the average mixed fertilizer weighs about one pound.

FERTILIZING DURING THE GROWING SEASON

During the growing season it may be necessary to sidedress two or three times with fertilizer at half the initial banded rate. Sidedressing refers to the practice of placing fertilizer in the soil beside your plants. To sidedress, make a 1-2 inch deep furrow down both sides of the row, 4-5 inches away from the plants. Uniformly distribute your fertilizer in the furrow and then cover the furrow with an inch or two of soil.

For plants such as watermelons, cantaloupes, cucumbers, and pumpkins, which are planted in widely spaced hills, sidedress in a circular furrow around the plants rather than down the rows.

Different vegetables differ in their fertilizer requirements. Some such as beans and southern peas are *light feeders* and may require no sidedressing. *Medium feeders* may require one or two sidedressings during their growth. Medium feeders include beets, cantaloupes, carrots, sweet corn, cucumber,

> *During the growing season it may be necessary to sidedress two or three times with fertilizer at half the initial banded rate.*

eggplant, greens (kale, collards, mustard, turnips, broccoli, cauliflower, and spinach), herbs, okra, English peas, peppers, pumpkins, radishes, rhubarb, Swiss chard, and watermelon. *Heavy feeders* may require 2-3 sidedressings. Heavy feeders include cabbage, celery, Irish potato, lettuce, onion, sweet potato, and tomato.

WATERING

Your vegetables need about 1 to 1½ inches of water per week during the warm growing season. On soils with a high clay content, one application of an inch of water any week that no rainfall is received should be adequate. On sandy soils, 2-3 applications of ½ inch each may be needed.

Any watering practice that wets the foliage favors disease development. Consider using soaker hoses rather than overhead sprinklers to keep the water off the foliage. There's a relatively new type of black soaker hose that leaks water out of thousands of tiny pores per inch of hose. It's more expensive than the traditional flat soaker hose that squirts water out of pin-sized holes. But, the hose (sometimes called 'leaky pipe') can be shallowly buried in the row and then lifted at the end of the season, to be used again the next season, season after season. Using this type of soaker hose is similar to using drip irrigation; the foliage will not be wet at all.

> *Your vegetables need about 1 to 1½ inches of water per week during the warm growing season.*

VARIETIES OF VEGETABLES

There are many different varieties of each type of vegetable (too many to list here). And, selecting the proper varieties can make a big difference. Call your county extension service office and ask if they can mail you a free copy of the recommended varieties for your area.

Stick with proven varieties for large plantings. You can always experiment with new varieties on a small scale until you learn how they perform.

SPACING OF VEGETABLES

Obviously, different types of plants require different spacings in the garden. When you call your county extension service office for variety recommendations, ask also that they send you a chart that gives recommended spacings for various vegetables. Such charts usually tell you how many seeds or plants will be needed to plant a given area of garden. It's great information and it's usually free to you if you'll only call and ask.

POLLINATION

Bees are very important in pollinating plants in the vegetable garden. Because bees are most active in the morning, apply any needed pesticides in the late afternoon or early evening. Use sprays rather than dusts, because the sprays, once dry, are less hazardous to the bees.

NEMATODE CONTROL

Nematodes are microscopic worms, some of which feed on plant roots. Most soils contain some plant parasitic nematodes, but populations are not always high enough to cause significant plant damage.

Nematode damage is less likely in soils with high levels of organic matter. So, continue to add available organic matter to your garden each year.

Nematode damage is also less likely in gardens where crops are rotated so that members of the same plant family are not planted in the same area of the garden year after year. For example, avoid planting tomatoes, eggplants, or peppers in the same spot of the garden in successive years. All these plants are in the Solanaceae family and would

> *Nematode damage is less likely in soils with high levels of organic matter. So, continue to add available organic matter to your garden each year. Nematode damage is also less likely in gardens where crops are rotated so that members of the same plant family are not planted in the same area of the garden year after year.*

be hosts to the same kinds of nematodes.

When nematode populations do become excessive, you may try *soil solarization*. This involves thoroughly cultivating the affected area in mid or late summer, removing clumps of plant debris, and then covering with clear plastic. If the plastic is left on for several weeks, the temperature beneath it will build to a level high enough to significantly reduce the nematode population.

There are no longer any soil fumigant nematacides that home gardeners can use for nematodes.

INSECT PEST CONTROL

Realize that not all insects you see in the garden are harmful. Many are harmless; others are actually beneficial pollinators or predators of pest insects.

You should check the garden closely for insect damage twice a week. When you find damage, spray only the affected plants. Follow pesticide label directions and precautions carefully.

Bacillus thuringiensis formulations such as Dipel®, Thuricide®, or Biotrol® can be used to control cabbage worms, tomato fruitworms, hornworms, pinworms, and squash vineborers. Commercial *soap pesticide* formulations such as Safer® Soap can be used to control aphids, spider mites, thrips, or whiteflies. Both these products, the soap and the B.T., are environmentally safe and good choices for the pests they control.

Malathion will control many insects: aphids, cabbageworms, cucumber beetles, leafhoppers, leafrollers, Mexican bean beetles, pea weevils, spider mites, stink bugs, and thrips.

Carbaryl (Sevin) will control: armyworms, budworms, cabbageworms, Colorado potato beetles, cucumber beetles, corn earworms, flea beetles, fruitworms, hornworms, pinworms, leafhoppers, pickleworms, melonworms, Mexican bean beetles, pea weevils, stink bugs, and thrips. Carbaryl is deadly to bees, though, so take care not to spray when bees are active. Also, use the liquid formulation of carbaryl rather than dusts to further safeguard bees. Once a spray dries, bees aren't likely to be poisoned by it. But carbaryl dust can get on the bee days later and poison not only the one bee but many more if he makes it back to the hive.

Diazinon will control: aphids, cabbageworms, leaf

miners, leafhoppers, leafrollers, Mexican bean beetles, pea weevils, spider mites, stink bugs, and thrips. A broadcast application of diazinon before planting the garden can be used to kill soil insects such as wireworms, cutworms, ants, and even mole crickets.

Baits containing Dylox or diazinon can be useful once the plants are up for controlling cutworms and mole crickets. Slug baits containing metaldehyde can be used for slug control, provided the label of the product says it's okay to use in a vegetable garden.

Never use any pesticide in a man-ner inconsistent with the label di-rections and precautions. Always wash the vegeta-bles from the garden before preparing or eating them.

DISEASE CONTROL

You're likely to always have some plant disease problems in the vegetable garden. But, you can reduce the incidence of disease problems by following several rules.

*R*ealize that not all insects you see in the garden are harmful. Many are harmless; others are actually beneficial pollinators or predators of pest insects.

Plant only disease-free, healthy plants in the garden. There's no need in introducing diseases into the garden on diseased plants!

Rotate the spot where you plant your garden each year if possible. If this isn't possible, at least try to rotate the spots where you plant specific types of vegetables in the garden. If you can't rotate, and if you had a problem with a particular soil-borne disease or a nematode in an area last year, fumigate before planting the following year. Use Vapam or Fume-V as discussed for nematodes.

Monitor your garden on a regular basis, at least twice a week. Remove diseased leaves or plants as they first show up. You can greatly slow disease spread.

Choose varieties resistant or tolerant to diseases when possible. Tomato varieties, for example, are often resistant to either verticillium wilt, fusarium wilt, or root-knot nematodes, as designated by the letters V, F, or N after the name of the variety.

Remember, though, that resistance is not infallible.

Plant fungicide-treated seed. Such seed is usually colored with a pink dye to indicate treatment. You can dust untreated seed with captan or thiram fungicide yourself before planting.

When a foliar disease starts in the garden, pick off affected leaves early. Sometimes you can stop the disease by doing so. But, often you'll have to resort to fungicide sprays so that you can prevent the rapid spread of the disease to other plants of the same type. For example, if a disease starts on beans, spray all the beans in that general area. The principle behind fungicide use is providing a protective coating on healthy leaves to prevent the spores of the disease from germinating and infecting them. Therefore, it pays to start the fungicide sprays before the disease becomes severe.

Fungicide sprays are generally more effective than dusts. Follow the fungicide labels completely. The label will tell on which plants you can use the fungicide, directions for mixing and applying, how soon you need to re-apply, how soon you can eat the vegetables after application, etc.

Chlorothalonil, maneb, and mancozeb are common fungicides that will control many *foliar vegetables diseases. Powdery mildews* can be controlled with triadimefon, sulfur, or benomyl. *Rusts* can be controlled with sulfur or ziram. Use basic copper sulfate plus maneb or mancozeb in controlling *bacterial spots*.

Be sure to only use formulations of any of these fungicides, though, which are labeled for use in vegetable gardens and on the particular types of vegetables you wish to spray. Follow all label directions and precautions very carefully. Never use a pesticide in any manner contrary to that specified on the label. If the pesticide label contradicts information in this book, follow the label information.

13
Birds

Add a New Dimension to Your Landscape

The activity of birds singing and moving about helps to make our home landscapes seem more like home. Yet, we can't take birds or other wildlife for granted. If we want them around, we must provide food, water, shelter and cover for them in our yards.

You may think that you can just put out a bird feeder and attract all the birds you want. It's not that simple, though. The birds want cover, shelter and water, also. For cover they need a mixture of trees, shrubs and plants of various sizes.

Think about it from the bird's view. You wouldn't hand around where there aren't plenty of places to hide from hawks or other predators. Nor, if you're a small bird, would you even want to hang out where you have to share your perch sites with larger, more raucous birds such as blue jays. Rather, you would want plenty of trees and shrubs around with room enough for everyone. Then, whenever the coast was clear, you could dart over to the bird feeder for a few seeds or to the bird bath for a drink of water.

It would also be great if there were some other sources of food, such as berries or seed on plants, besides the bird feeder. If you're a ground feeder, such as towhee or a brown thrasher, you don't even care about the bird feeder. You want a good mulch of leaves, pine straw, or other organic material at the base of shrub beds so that you can forage for food and be reasonably well hidden.

And, finally from the bird's view, you must have a nesting site nearby if you're to make this home. Depending on the type of bird you are, the nesting site could be anything from a large shrub or small tree to a cavity in an old dead pine tree.

If you wish to encourage a diversity of birds in your yard, then you must have a diversity of food, nesting sites and cover. A homesite with a large lawn, a few small, tightly clipped shrubs and a couple of large shade threes won't attract that many birds. But a homesite with a diversity of large trees, some understory trees, evergreen and deciduous trees, neat but not formally sheared medium to large hedges and shrubs, and a not-so-large lawn is much more likely to attract a diversity of birds.

Many of the plants that are attractive to birds are also attractive to other small animals such as raccoons, opossums, foxes, and, of course, squirrels. So, there is the added benefit of being able to watch these animals, too.

> **Y**ou may think that you can just put out a bird feeder and attract all the birds you want. It's not that simple, though. The birds want cover, shelter and water, also. For cover they need a mixture of trees, shrubs and plants of various sizes.

SOME LANDSCAPE PLANTS ATTRACTIVE TO BIRDS

SHRUBS AND SMALL TO MEDIUM TREES

Red Buckeye (Aesculus pavia): A small native deciduous shrub that blooms in the spring with red tubular flowers liked by hummingbirds. Needs partial shade.

American beautyberry (Calicarpa americana): This small native deciduous shrub produces bright purple berries in clusters on the stem, ripening in the late summer to fall. If pruned a little during the early growing season to make it a little bushier, it can be an attractive landscape addition as a small shrub. Many birds such as mockingbirds, woodpeckers and cardinals like the berries.

Hackberry or Sugarberry (Celtis laevigata): Medium to large deciduous native tree. Many birds eat the fruit.

Fringe tree (Chionanthus virginicus): A small, native deciduous tree that flowers in mid-spring with flossy, white clouds of flowers. Many birds eat the fruit that follows on the female plants.

Flowering dogwood (Cornus florida): One of our most favored and attractive of small deciduous native trees. Beautiful spring flowers, great fall leaf color, and bright red berries which are loved by many birds in winter!

Hawthorn (Crataegus spp.): Small, thorny, deciduous tree. Beautiful flowers in spring; often great fall color! Fruit eaten by some birds. Native.

Dahoon holly (Ilex cassine): Another evergreen native holly with red berries liked by birds. Leaves usually spineless.

Possumhaw (Ilex decidua): Small, native deciduous holly. Attractive red berries on female plants are attractive food for many birds.

American holly (Ilex opaca): Somewhat slender, upright native evergreen tree. Females produce typical red holly berries eaten by many birds. There are several hybrids of American holly, including 'Savannah' and 'East Palatka.'

Yaupon (Ilex vomitoria): A small, evergreen native holly tree. Females produce small red berries attractive to birds. Buy only plants specified in the nursery as female. There is a new weeping cultivar available, too, but it probably wouldn't be as inviting to birds because of branch structure.

Southern red cedar (Juniperus silicicola): Evergreen native tree, producing small blue fruit attractive to many birds. The density of the cedar makes it a good nest site for many birds and a good screening plant for landscape purposes. Relatively fast-growing. Medium in size.

Oregon grape holly (Mahonia bealei): Medium evergreen shrub with thick, spiny leaves. Clusters of blue berries are especially attractive to mockingbirds. For shade to sun.

Crabapple (Malus angustifolia): Attractive small, flowering, deciduous tree with fruit attractive to several birds.

Wax myrtle (Myrica cerifera): Be sure to buy only plants specified as female plants; only they produce the berries eaten by many birds. Yellow-rumped warblers, ruby-crowned kinglets, and others like the waxy gray berries. I enjoy watching cardinals nest in a wax myrtle by my home office window each year. Wax myrtles can be trained as hedges, small trees, or large shrubs, reaching 10 feet or so in height if desired. Though some people aren't excited by wax myrtles (they're such a common native), they're one of our most adaptable and versatile landscape plants.

American hornbeam (Ostrya virginiana): Small deciduous native tree. Nuts eaten by some birds.

Cherry laurel (Prunus caroliniana): Fast-growing shiny-leafed evergreen small tree that makes a good hedge or an attractive single plant. Many birds attracted to the fruit in winter. Native. Biggest drawback is that it sprouts easily wherever birds spread the seeds.

Black cherry or wild cherry (Prunus serotina): The black fruit from this slender, medium-size native deciduous tree provides food for many birds in the summer. Eastern tent caterpillar webs infest the tree most every spring but do not cause permanent damage. The leaves grow back, and the caterpillars provide food for the yellow-billed cuckoo.

Pyracantha (Pyracantha spp.): A non-native cascading shrub with thorns and beautiful orange berries in the fall. Needs plenty of room and full sun. Mockingbirds love the berries and tend to stake out territory in pyracantha bushes.

Blackberry (Rubus spp.): Another fruit that both you and the birds can enjoy. Cut back old canes just after harvest season to keep them productive and neat. Needs full sun. The new named varieties offer larger berries than our wild berries.

Elderberry (Sambucus canadensis): Though not usually thought of as a landscape plant, this large native shrub, producing clusters of cream-colored flowers in spring and berries following, is attractive to many birds. Could be useful in the landscape.

Sassafras (Sassafras albidum): Medium-sized native deciduous tree. Females have dark blue fruit attractive to birds. Good purplish red fall leaf color. Attractive tree that should be planted more.

Winged elm (Ulmus alata): Good small to medium native shade tree. Deciduous. Seed liked by many birds.

Blueberry (Vaccinium spp.): The blueberry can make an attractive hedge, though it is deciduous (losing its leaves in winter). It will provide fruit for you and many birds. See the chapter on fruit for more information on selecting blueberry cultivars. Needs full sun.

LARGER TREES

Maples, red and Florida (Acer rubrum and A. saccharum var. Floridanum or A. barbatum): Winged seeds eaten by some birds. Red maple has bright red seeds in spring. Both red maple and Florida sugar maple have attractive fall color. Natives.

Hickory (Carya spp.): Nuts eaten by blue jays, woodpeckers and crows. These stately deciduous trees have the most striking gold foliage! Natives.

Persimmon (Diospyros virginiana): The native persimmon gets quite large with time, unlike the Oriental persimmons we often plant for fruit. Fruit of the native persimmon are smaller and very astringent until quite ripe. Are attractive to birds and other wildlife.

American beech (Fagus grandifolia): Nuts liked by many birds. Magnificent large native tree with beautiful whitish bark. Gold fall foliage. Brown leaves hang on tree into winter.

Sweetgum (Liquidambar styraciflua): Tall, slender deciduous tree with very attractive fall color. Seeds borne in the spiny sweetgum balls liked by many birds. Native. Becomes quite tall with time.

Southern magnolia (Magnolia grandiflora): Birds like the red seeds. Good cover for birds, too. Evergreen native. White flowers in early summer.

Red mulberry (Morus rubra): The berries of the female trees attract many types of birds. Fruit can be messy, so don't plant overhanging roof, patio, driveway, etc. Native.

Black gum (Nyssa sylvatica): Blue fruit eaten by birds such as woodpeckers, cardinals, blue jays, etc. Hollows in old trees make nest sites for some birds. Red to orange fall leaf color on this native.

Pines (Pinus spp.): Including natives loblolly, spruce, shortleaf, longleaf, pond, slash and sand pines. All are evergreen. Seeds provide food for many birds. Trees provide cover and nest sites.

Oaks (Quercus spp.): Includes natives live oaks, white oaks, laurel oaks, water oaks, Shumard oaks, southern red oaks and others. All are deciduous except live and laurel oaks. Acorns provide food. Trees provide cover, nest sites and insects for food.

Sabal palm or cabbage palm (Sabal palmetto): The black berries serve as food for a variety of birds. One of the more cold-hardy palms. Native to much of our region.

VINES

Trumpet vine (Campsis radicans): The orange flowers of this deciduous native vine are very attractive to hummingbirds.

Coral honeysuckle (Lonicera sempervirens): Red flowers of this deciduous native vine attract hummingbirds.

Virginia creeper (Parthenocissus quinquefolia): Small dark berries of this deciduous native vine serve as food for many birds. This vine is often confused with poison ivy, but Virginia creeper has five leaflets, not three as does poison ivy. Turns a beautiful red in fall. Poison ivy, incidentally, also has berries eaten by many birds.

BIRD FEEDERS IN THE LANDSCAPE

Obviously, bird feeders attract birds. Some birds can even be drawn into relatively barren areas when you supply them with preferred food on a regular basis. But, bird feeders work best when you also provide the other aspects of

> *Place the feeder so that there is cover to escape predators within 10-20 feet from the feeder. But don't place the feeder right in the midst of thick shrubbery or other such cover where a cat could sneak up unseen.*

the birds' preferred habit. The cover, nesting sites, water and feed are all important if you wish to permanently increase the diversity of birds around your landscape.

You can enjoy feeding birds year-round. You'll find different birds there during different seasons of the year. Don't worry, though, if you don't have food in the feeders all the time. Though the birds will become accustomed to finding feed in your feeders, rarely is there a shortage of feed in the wild this far south, even in inclement weather. So the birds can survive even without your feed.

Your bird feeder should protect the seed from getting wet. Wet seed will spoil quickly and can be harmful to the birds.

Place the feeder so that there is cover to escape predators within 10-20 feet from the feeder. But don't place the feeder right in the midst of thick shrubbery or other such cover where a cat could sneak up unseen.

It's best not to mix different kinds of seed in one feeder. The birds will pick out their favorites and the rest will fall to the ground where it sprouts and becomes weedy. So avoid many of the commercial seed mixtures.

Sunflower seeds are a favorite of many birds. Cardinals, goldfinches, purple finches, woodpeckers, titmice, chickadees, blue jays, doves and even wrens, will visit feeders with sunflower seeds.

You may reduce visits by less desirable or nuisance species to your feeder if you keep their favorite foods out of the feeder. For instance, wheat is preferred by house sparrows.

Squirrels can be a nuisance also. The most effective 'squirrel-proof' feeder I've found is a metal pole with the wide saucer-shaped squirrel baffle/feeding platform that fits around it. A perch feeder mounts on top of the pole over the squirrel baffle/feeding platform. Even this type of feeder has to be in an open spot out of jumping distance of squirrels (8-10 feet).

There are also squirrel baffles available for hanging feeders. And there are poles with sliding spring-loaded sections designed to keep squirrels from climbing them. If you live in an urban area and don't want to share the bird seed with squirrels, you'll have to use one of the squirrel-proof mechanisms.

A *suet feeder* will attract some birds that may not come to a seed feeder. For example, mockingbirds will come to a suet feeder. Raw suet (beef fat) will become rancid quickly, so either buy suet cakes from a store that sells them for bird-feeding, or you can make your own.

To make suet cakes, melt a cup of ground suet in a saucepan. Blend in a cup of smooth peanut butter. In a separate bowl, mix together 2-3 cups of yellow corn meal and ½ cup of enriched or whole wheat flour. When the suet/peanut butter mixture has cooled and started thickening, blend in the dry ingredients. Pour the mixture into a flat cake pan and cut into cakes when hardened. Or, pour the mixture into muffin tins. Use the suet cakes in suet feeders. Or, an alternative would be to stuff the thickened suet mixture into pine cones for hardening there. The cones could then be used as suet feeders. (Note: If squirrels are a problem, you may wish to delete the peanut butter from the recipe.)

Hummingbird feeders are typically used to attract hummingbirds. Of course, many flowers are useful in attracting hummingbirds, too. But the feeders, which you fill with sugar water and hang so that the red color of the feeders are visible, often attract quite a few hummingbirds.

Be sure to buy a hummingbird feeder that can easily be cleaned with vinegar water each week. It's important to keep the feeders clean. Try not to place the feeders in direct sun.

To mix the sugar solution for the feeders, dissolve one quarter cup of white, granulated sugar per cup of boiling water. Let the solution cool to room temperature (or put it in the refrigerator to cool it more quickly) before filling the feeders. Don't add red food coloring to the solution. It hasn't been proven definitely that it causes health problems for the hummingbirds, but there is a possibility. And it isn't needed to attract the birds. The red color of the feeder is sufficient attraction. So, leave out the food color to play it safe.

Hummingbirds migrate to the tropics for the winter. So, you'll only have hummingbirds during the spring, summer and early fall.

WATER

There's more to supplying water for birds than just buying a bird-bath and occasionally filling it.

Be picky about the birdbath you buy; if the sides are too steep, the birds won't use it for bathing. The water needs to gradually slope out to its deepest point of 2-3 inches so that the birds can wade in.

First, be picky about the birdbath you buy; if the sides are too steep, the birds won't use it for bathing. The water needs to gradually slope out to its deepest point of 2-3 inches so that the birds can wade in.

The birds prefer a shaded spot, protected, about 15 feet from shrubbery and three feet off the ground.

The sound of dripping or misting water will help insure that the birds find the water. Consider rigging up a mist of water that shoots up into an overhanging tree and drips back into the birdbath. Birds are most active from sunrise to 10 a.m. and from late afternoon to shortly after sunset. You could install a timer at the hose outlet to turn the mister on and off at those times.

Finally, keep the water clean. This will benefit both the birds and you, too, as mosquitoes will breed in unchanged birdbaths. And, make sure that water's always there on a dependable basis.

BIRD HOUSES

Birds that nest in cavities in trees, branches, or fence posts often have a difficult time finding enough nest sites in developed urban areas. Bird houses can provide such birds with nest sites.

When building or buying a bird house, make sure it is properly designed for the particular species of bird you wish to attract. Birds are picky about their nest sites.

According to a booklet published by the Florida Nongame Wildlife Program, "*Planting a Refuge for Wildlife,*" bluebirds prefer houses with a floor of about 5x5 inches. The walls should be about eight inches high. And the entrance hole should be 1½ inches in diameter and six inches above the floor. The house should be positioned 5-10 feet above the ground.

If you live in an urban area without any wide-open fields, you probably won't get bluebirds, though. But you can attract birds such as Carolina wrens, purple martins, chickadees and woodpeckers with appropriately designed houses.

A house for a red-bellied or red-headed woodpecker, though, obviously needs to be larger than a bluebird house. Build the floor 6x6 inches, the walls 15 inches tall, and the entrance hole two inches in diameter and nine inches above the floor. Put 3-4 inches of sawdust in the box and position it 8-20 feet above the ground.

When building bird houses, it's wise to slant the top to provide better rain runoff. And design the back or top so that it will hinge open for cleaning in between nestings. Otherwise, mites can become a problem for the birds.

Build bird houses of $^3/_4$ inch durable woods such as cypress, western cedar or exterior-grade plywood. Use rough-cut lumber; it will give the birds a foothold when they are entering and exiting. Never use metal or plastic; they absorb heat and may kill the young birds. An exception to this is in the case of the anodized aluminum purple martin houses. These houses are properly ventilated to allow cooling.

Never use metal or plastic; they absorb heat and may kill the young birds. An exception to this is the case of the anodized aluminum purple martin houses. These houses are properly ventilated to allow cooling.

Any good bird house should have a gap or ventilation holes under the roof overhang. The house should also have drainage holes.

14
Pruning

Why, When and How

Pruning is an important part of landscape maintenance. Yet, it is the most misunderstood and neglected part of landscape maintenance.

WHEN TO PRUNE

Just before spring growth begins is an excellent time to do most pruning. The major exception is with *spring-flowering plants* such as azaleas. Wait until they finish blooming to prune them so that you don't prune off the long-awaited flowers that have formed on last year's growth.

Summer-flowering plants, on the other hand, need to be pruned in late winter or early spring if you prune them. They'll form flower buds on the new growth that pops out in early spring. Oleander and crape myrtle are good examples.

Deciduous shade trees are usually pruned during the late fall or winter after they drop their leaves. *Fruit trees*, as already discussed in the chapter on fruit trees, are pruned in January or February.

PRUNING STEP-BY-STEP

Why do you prune a plant? There are several reasons. First, you need to *remove wood that is dead, weak, damaged, diseased or insect-infested.* Second, you need to *remove branches that are rubbing against each other.* Third, you need to *remove branches that are growing in the wrong direction* (such as branches

growing toward each other and that will soon be rubbing branches).

Next, you sometimes need to *remove tired old branches and allow new ones to grow* (nandina is a good example). Another reason for pruning is when you wish to *train a plant into a certain shape or form.* Training a formal boxwood hedge or training a peach tree to an open center are examples. And finally, you often prune just to *maintain a plant at a certain size.* It's best to plant the type of plant that will achieve the desired size with the least amount of pruning. But sometimes pruning is needed for size control.

Regardless of all the reasons for pruning, there are basically only two types of pruning cuts you can make.

HOW DIFFERENT TYPES OF PRUNING CUTS ACHIEVE DIFFERENT RESULTS

Regardless of all the reasons for pruning, there are basically only two types of pruning cuts you can make. But which type of these two pruning cuts you use determines the result achieved. If you use the wrong type of cut, you will not achieve the desired result.

The first major type of pruning cut is the *thinning*

cut. A thinning cut is when you remove an entire limb all the way back to the main trunk or to another major limb. No new growth results from a thinning cut.

The other major type of pruning cut is what is often referred to as a *'heading-back' cut*. When 'heading back,' you cut back just part of a small branch. This destroys the growth dominance of the end of the cut branch and causes buds or limbs behind the cut to begin growing. A 'heading-back' cut, therefore, thickens the plant.

You may be thinking, then, that a heading-back cut is good because it thickens the plant. Sometimes it is good; sometimes it's not. Sometimes a plant is so thick on the surface that it has no interior growth. Such a plant can benefit from thinning so that light can reach further into the plant. Too much thickness also results in a lot of cross-over and rubbing branches, which also are undesirable.

Heading-back cuts should not be used on large limbs. Don't use heading back cuts on large limbs when the lateral limbs are not at least one-third the size of the limb being headed back.

WHEN TO HEAD-BACK AND WHEN TO THIN

So, there are times to head-back and times to thin. Suppose, for instance, you're trying to get a new redtop hedge to fill in. You may head-back growth frequently (after each new flush of growth hardens off) in order to make the hedge fuller. At the same time, though, you need to make some thinning cuts to remove branches that will soon become crossing or rubbing branches.

A year or two later you will definitely find the redtop hedge in need of some thinning to remove such cross-over or rubbing branches. Many old plants could benefit tremendously from some judicious thinning.

In fact, most older plants really need little heading-back. One of the major reasons for heading-back growth on an older plant is to reduce its size. So, if you put the plant in a spot where it has plenty of room to grow, you'll only have to do a little heading-back to induce lanky branches to fill out. Most of your cuts will be thinning cuts.

MAKING THE PRUNING CUT . . . AND, SHOULD YOU USE PRUNING PAINT?

For years horticulturists and arborists encouraged the use of pruning paints or tree dressings to cover pruning cuts larger than the size of a quarter. The most recent research, however, shows no advantage to covering pruning wounds with such a material.

On the contrary, such pruning paints and dressings could even seal in moisture, making conditions more favorable for disease organisms. The current recommendation is just that you make a good, clean pruning cut so that the plant can quickly seal off the wound itself.

If you're removing a limb, never, never leave a long stub off the trunk when you make your pruning cut.

If you're removing a limb, never, never leave a long stub off the trunk when you make your pruning cut. Instead, cut back to just outside the ridge of bark that attaches the limb to the trunk or larger limb. Your cut should not be so flush to the trunk that no protrusion at all is left. Yet, neither should a long stub be left.

Similarly, if you're cutting back a limb to a point where a lateral limb branches off, be sure to cut the main limb back fairly close to the point where the lateral limb branches off. Don't leave a long stub extending beyond the lateral branch.

HEDGE SHEARING

Hedge shearing involves primarily all heading-back cuts. Hedge shearing is permissible on certain small-leafed plants, such as boxwood hedge, where a formal appearance is desired. But, shearing is an unwise and overused practice on many other shrubs. Frequent shearing results in dense growth on the surface of the plant. But the interior of the plant often develops into a tangled mess of bare crossing and rubbing branches with few leaves. If injury ever occurs to a portion of the surface foliage, a gaping hole is left in the plant.

Try to use a combination of thinning and heading-back cuts on most plants. The results will usually be a more feathery, natural-looking plant and a healthier plant. And you'll have to prune much less often than if you had sheared the planting into a formal hedge. Formal hedges require monthly or bi-monthly pruning to keep them formal.

PRUNING OVERGROWN SHRUBS

The ideal situation is to plant the proper plant for a given spot - a plant that will never outgrow its site and will only require light pruning to keep it in shape. In reality, though, we often have shrubs that outgrow their spot and that begin hiding windows or crowding entrances. How do you prune such plants?

Often home gardeners try to solve the problem by cutting the shrubs back to about half their size. The result, though, is often oddly shaped plants which usually grow back to their original height by the end of the first growing season.

Drastic pruning is usually a better solution. Many overgrown shrubs can be rejuvenated by cutting them back to within 6-12 inches of the ground. This is one case in which it is acceptable to use heading back cuts on large limbs.

Most broadleaf shrubs, such as azaleas, Chinese and Japanese hollies, camellias, pittosporums, gardenias, nandinas and abelieas, respond well to such drastic pruning if their root system is healthy and vigorous. Provided you prune at the proper time, a healthy plant has about a 90 percent chance of recovery. Weak, diseased plants often die as a result of severe pruning.

Late February to mid-March, before new growth begins, is the best time for severe pruning.

Some types of plants will not tolerate such severe pruning. Boxwoods, for example, recover extremely slowly from drastic pruning, taking years if they recover at all.

Narrow-leaf or needle evergreens, such as junipers, should not be pruned drastically. Such plants have few dormant buds beneath the bark of old wood and will usually die from severe pruning. It is best to remove such overgrown plants.

On those plants you can rejuvenate by severe

Hedge shearing is permissible on certain small-leafed plants, such as a boxwood hedge, where a formal appearance is desired. But, shearing is an unwise and overused practice on many other shrubs.

pruning, use clean cuts. A pruning saw is usually needed to cut the large limbs at their base. Sterilize the pruning tools with alcohol frequently to prevent the spread of disease organisms from diseased to healthy wood.

After pruning back an overgrown plant, be sure to give it the best of care if you expect it to recover. Water plants weekly during dry weather. Make sure there is a two-inch layer of mulch, such as pine straw, extending well beyond the base of the plant. Fertilize at a normal rate for the original plant size (two teaspoons of 16-4-8 per foot of plant height in March, May and July).

Growth will be slow at first. It may take 4-6 weeks before the new buds break through the bark. But after that, growth will come quickly, provided there are ample nutrients and moisture for the plant.

As the new shoots elongate, you may find that they are very long and lanky. You will need to tip-prune shoots when they become 6-12 inches long so that side branches will develop. Do this several times during the growing season so that a more compact plant is formed. At the same time, you will need to remove many of the new shoots to prevent overcrowding.

Late February to mid-March, before new growth begins, is the best time for severe pruning.

PRUNING ROSES

If you have rose bushes in your landscape, January or February is the time to bring out the pruning tools and give the roses their heavy annual pruning. Pruning is necessary to get the best flowering performance from your plants the following flowering season.

Before you do any cutting, you should remove the mulch around the base of the bush and look at the overall condition of the plant. If the overall bush is not very vigorous and the base of the plant is severely knotted, scarred, or otherwise injured, you may wish to discard the bush. All the pruning in the world won't perform miracles on an unhealthy bush.

But if the overall health of the plant appears OK, your first step is to remove all dead and spindly growth back to the base of the bush. Keep only the strong, stocky, healthy canes.

Even some of the strong canes may need to be removed if they're growing toward the center of the bush. Your objective is to open up the middle of the bush by directing growth to the outside. If there is too much growth in the center of the bush, sunlight cannot penetrate and pest organisms are provided with a haven by the thick growth.

Retain only four to six strong canes, depending on the vigor and the growth habits of the bush. Keep a lower number of canes on less vigorous plants and more on plants that don't grow so fast. Try to leave no canes smaller in diameter than a pencil.

When you make the cuts to remove canes, cut all the way back to the base. Don't leave stubs. Stubs won't heal and will provide entry points for disease and insect pests.

Once you've removed all unnecessary canes, then you shorten the remaining canes to about knee height. When you prune back canes, look for an outwardly facing bud. Make your pruning cut about a quarter inch above that bud. Make the cut at a 45 degree angle with the high side of the cut on the same side of the branch as the bud. If the center of the stem is not a healthy light color, look for another outwardly facing bud six inches or so lower and make another cut. Before making this second cut, though, be sure to sterilize your clippers with alcohol.

Pruning should encourage new canes to come from the base of the rose plant and from the canes that are left. Don't be so overly concerned about making mistakes that you totally avoid pruning. Rose bushes are forgiving plants and, if healthy, will survive your mistakes. But they need your pruning to give best performance.

Be sure to use sharp pruning clippers and loppers. You may need a small pruning saw to remove large canes. If you don't have the proper tools, buy them. You'll need them for other pruning jobs around the landscape.

PRUNING CRAPE MYRTLES

Pruning crape myrtles follows the same principles as pruning most other plants. Just as you wished to open up the center of the rose and remove crossing and rubbing branches, you'll need to do the same for crape myrtles. Then remove all twiggy or weak growth and water sprouts. Remove the tips of the limbs holding last year's seed pods.

Some people wish to prune crape myrtles back severely, training them more as bushes rather than trees. If that's your preference, it is certainly permissible. But don't prune crape myrtles as bushes just because that's the way you've always seen it done. The taller tree form of crape myrtle is just as acceptable, and, in fact, more in vogue today. The tree form also shows off the crape myrtle's beautiful gnarled trunks during the dormant season.

15

House Plants

Growing Plants Indoors

Though this book is primarily about growing plants outdoors in the landscape, I thought it worthwhile to include a brief section about growing plants indoors. So many people enjoy house plants.

Unfortunately, though, growing plants indoors can be difficult, especially if you don't understand the factors in the indoor environment that make it so. The primary factors which cause difficulty in growing plants indoors are low light levels, low humidity levels and water or soil moisture management.

LIGHT LEVELS

Simply put, the light levels in most places inside most homes are not adequate for the growth of most plants. But then there are locations such as south, east, or west-facing windows that have quite a bit of light - even too much for some house plants.

So, one of the keys to growing house plants is selecting ones suitable for the light levels with which you are dealing. Examples of plants for low light areas are *Aglaonema, Aspidistra, Chamaedorea palms* and *Sansevieria.*

Plants for high light areas include *Philodendron selloum, African violets, Areca palm, Ficus benjamina* and *Norfolk Island pine*.

Plants for 'average' light areas include most of the *ferns, schefflera, Dieffenbachia, Dracaenas, pothos, Ficus pumila,* and *nephthytis,* among others.

HUMIDITY

With air conditioning and heating, the air inside most homes simply does not contain enough moisture to be favorable to the growth of most plants. Possible solutions are buying a humidifier or misting the plants with a mist bottle every day or so.

WATER AND SOIL MOISTURE MANAGEMENT

It's often been said that the most common cause of house plant death is overwatering. Overwatering robs the soil of another critical component, oxygen. So the plant roots die.

When growing house plants, it's best to use a soil mixture that drains quickly. You can always add more water to a well-drained soil mix. But a soil mix that holds too much water will stay wet for long periods of time, depriving the plant roots of needed oxygen.

Pre-bagged soil mixes aren't always well-drained enough. If a mix seems too 'heavy' or poorly drained, you may add ingredients such as perlite to improve the drainage.

Also, all plant containers need to have drainage holes to allow excess water to escape.

How often should you water? It's impossible to

With most plants, you should water as soon as the soil becomes dry to the touch.

answer that question here because there are so many factors involved, from time of year, to type of plant to type of soil mix. You have to be willing to stick your finger in the soil from time to time to feel how dry it's getting.

With most plants, you want to water as soon as the soil becomes dry to the touch. Water thoroughly, until water runs out the drainage hole at the bottom. You may have to take the plant outside to water or put it over the sink. Or, if the plant has a saucer under it, you may water until water runs into it. However, empty the saucer after watering. Don't allow the plant to stand in the water-filled saucer.

Don't water again until the soil becomes dry again. A few plants (you'll just have to learn these as you go) like for the soil to stay a little more moist. And a few plants (cacti being a prime example) can go for much longer periods between waterings.

Signs of underwatering are generally browning of the leaf tips and margins. However, the signs of overwatering can be the same because overwatering damages the root system, which is required to take up water.

FERTILIZING

Most house plants don't grow rapidly. So they don't need a whole lot of fertilizer. Don't overdo it.

There are many commercial house plant fertilizers. Most do a good job when used as directed.

Depending on the type of fertilizer used, you'll normally only need to fertilize every month or two during the warmer months. During the winter or when growing plants under low light conditions, you'll need to fertilize much less. One fertilization may get the plants through the winter.

16
New Plants
& Products You Should Try

One of the major trends in gardening today is toward a lower-maintenance, more environmentally friendly garden. Gardeners simply don't have the time or the desire to grow plants that require frequent sprays, watering or other care. Yet, we want attractive gardens, and we have more and more attractive plants from which to choose.

ANNUAL FLOWERS

Several annuals that were relatively unknown ten years ago are becoming more and more popular because of their ability to stand up to our summer heat and humidity:

Melampodium paludosum is an extremely fast-growing, heat-tolerant annual for sun or light shade. Each small plant set out in spring can grow to become a two-foot plant by mid-summer, covered with small yellow flowers. In addition, new plants will continually sprout at the base from the seeds dropped by the parent plant. *Melampodium* is also one of few annual flowers that can be started in the middle of summer and be expected to tolerate the heat. It's just a really dependable annual for the flower garden.

Zinnia angustifolia (formerly Z. linearis) is another tough annual flower that's winning many admirers. Available in either orange-yellow or white, this 1-2 foot zinnia with small flowers takes our heat and humidity well and is very drought-tolerant. Try

some in a sunny spot and you'll like it!

Though many gardeners know *Gomphrena globosa (globe amaranth)*, many more should know it. Heat- and drought-tolerant, this annual produces clover-like blooms of pink, purple, red, lavender or white (depending on cultivar) all summer. In addition, the flowers are useful in arrangements and for drying. It's for full sun to partial shade.

PERENNIAL FLOWERS

Barleria cristata (Phillipine violet) gains new admirers every fall when it flowers. Growing to a height of 3-4 feet over the spring and summer, the bushy plant suddenly becomes loaded with purple flowers in fall. This plant performs well in full sun to partial shade.

Cuphea micropetala (Cigar flower) is one of those perennials you can just about plant and forget. However, you'll be reminded of it in fall when its small yellow and orange, cigar-shaped flowers cover the three-foot bush. Very drought-tolerant, this plant prefers full sun for best flowering.

Dianthus 'First Love' is one of the most floriferous and showiest of the dianthuses. Producing loads of mildly fragrant flowers of white and various shades of pink on two-foot stems perfect for cutting, this plant has quickly become one of my favorites. It's too early for me to say whether it will be a reliable perennial here. But even if it's not, it will be a wonderful fall, winter and spring annual.

Salvia x 'Indigo Spires' is a perennial everyone should have in their perennial garden. Long indigo flower spikes appear from May until frost. The flower color is very intense in the fall, even iridescent. This salvia is such a vigorous grower, it will require cutting back at least once during the growing season. Otherwise, it will reach 4-5 feet tall, become very lanky, and fall over if not staked. Cutting back in mid-to-late summer sends forth new growth and new flowers in fall. It does best in full sun.

Solidago rugosa 'Fireworks' is a new goldenrod released by Niche Gardens, Chapel Hills, N.C., in cooperation with the North Carolina Botanical Gardens. It is clump-forming rather than spreading from underground stems, so it shouldn't be invasive like some goldenrods. It can grow to 3-4 feet tall, preferring moist sites in full sun. Its branches are arching, becoming covered with golden yellow flowers in the fall.

Verbena 'Homestead Purple' is a verbena discovered on an old homesite between Athens and Atlanta by University of Georgia horticulturist, Allan Armitage. With an extremely brilliant purple flower, this verbena grows vigorously and flowers continuously throughout spring and summer. Heat and humidity sometimes may get the best of it at the end of the summer, preventing it from carrying through the winter, especially if it's not in a well-drained enough spot. But, even if it does die then, it's worth planting as an annual. It's that showy!

VINES

Bignonia capreolata (cross-vine) is a native evergreen vine which produces orange flowers primarily in spring. It can wrap its tendrils around a trellis or pole, but it can also attach itself to a masonry or brick wall, yet not damage the wall. A few nurseries are now selling this very good native vine. One particular cultivar, 'Tangerine Beauty,' is noted for its numerous ruby-tangerine flowers.

Campsis grandiflora (Chinese trumpet creeper) is the Asian counterpart of our native trumpetcreeper, *Campsis radicans*. It is less invasive than the native trumpetcreeper, yet is especially floriferous, producing many 2-3-inch wide apricot flowers for two months in early summer. It then flowers sporadically through the rest of the summer if the seed pods are removed.

Clematis armandii is an evergreen vine for shaded gardens. Beautiful dark green, slender, leathery leaves are accented by a sprinkling of white blooms in late winter or early spring.

SHRUBS

Clethra alnifolia (summersweet or sweet pepper bush) is a fragrant summer-flowering native with white flowers. Leaves turn yellow to orange in the fall before dropping. Clethra is a good shrub for shade or sun. Selected cultivars have characteristics superior to the native parent. 'Hummingbird' is noted for its compact, dwarf habit to about four feet tall, and heavy crops of white flowers. 'Fern Valley Pink' has vivid pink flowers in racemes up to a foot long. 'Pink Spire' also has pink flowers. 'Rosea' has rose colored flowers.

Itea virginica (Virginia sweetspire) is another deciduous native shrub, becoming increasingly popular for its beautiful fall color. Growing in sun to partial shade, *Itea* typically reaches five feet tall. White flowers appear in late spring to summer. 'Henry's Garnet' is a selection noted for its six-inch flowers and brilliant red fall color.

Dwarf crape myrtles are seeing more and more use in landscapes and in container plantings. They provide summer flowers and fall foliage color. 'New Orleans' is a very dwarf (two-foot) cultivar with superb purple flowers. 'Bayou Marie' has medium pink flowers and will grow to four feet tall in time. 'Baton Rouge' has dark pink flowers.

The *althea* or *rose-of-Sharon, Hibiscus syriacus,* is another old-time favorite that's now offered in several improved cultivars. Typically, the new cultivars offer showier and larger flowers. 'Aphrodite' has deep rose-pink flowers with a deep red eye. 'Diana' has six-inch white flowers. 'Helene' has 3-4 inch white flowers with a burgundy eye. 'Minerva' has 4-5 inch lavender-violet flowers with a burgundy eye.

Loropetalum Chinese (evergreen witchhazel) is a shrub that's been used in southern landscapes for years because of its feathery white flowers in spring. But several new cultivars are improvements over the traditional species. 'Blush' has new leaves that are burgundy, fading to green, and pink flowers. 'Burgundy' has new foliage that is burgundy, fading to burgundy-green, and pink flowers. A variety called rubrum has leaves that stay medium burgundy. Its flowers are hot pink. Loropetalums prefer filtered shade.

TREES

Acer barbatum (Florida sugar maple), though not new, is still not well-known and is relatively new to the nursery trade. A small maple with gorgeous yellow fall color, this tree should be used more.

Seed-propagated trees of *Acer rubrum (red maple)* are used often in landscaping. Yet, fall color is not always good because there is a lot of seedling variation. Based on trials by Auburn University, the following cultivars have consistently good red fall color in mid-Alabama: 'Autumn Flame,' 'Bowhall,' 'Gerling,' and 'Tilford.' Quite possibly, these cultivars would be good choices for our area also.

Cercis chinensis 'Avondale' is a spectacular redbud new to the nursery trade. It's an upright multi-stemmed shrub or small tree which flowers in late winter a little earlier than our native redbud. The pink flowers literally cover the branches.

Chionanthus retusus (Chinese fringe tree) is considered a better choice than our native fringe tree, *C. virginicus*, because the flowers are fuller. The tree also grows a little larger than the native fringe tree.

The *Gresham hybrid magnolias* offer even more spectacular deciduous, late winter flowering magnolias than we're accustomed to with the *Magnolia soulangiana (saucer magnolia)*. Examples of selections are 'Royal Crown, 'Pink Goblet,' 'Winelight,' and 'Jon Jon.'

Prunus mume (flowering apricot) is a large shrub or small tree typically flowering in January or February. The Japanese consider it to be superior to the flowering cherry. Improved cultivars include 'Bonita' (rose-red semi-double flowers), 'Dawn' (ruffled light pink), 'Matsurabara Red' (double red), 'Peggy Clarke' (double rose pink), and 'Rosemary Clark' (double white).

VEGETABLES

Big Beef F1 hybrid tomato is a large tomato with full flavor, improved disease resistance, increased vigor and high yield. It won a 1994 All-America Selections Award.

Fanfare F1 cucumber, also a 1994 All-America

Award Winner, produces 8-9 inch cucumbers even after other varieties have quit. Though an abundant producer, the plants are compact. It's good for containers or small gardens. Fanfare has good disease resistance.

NEW PRODUCTS

BETTER FOR THE ENVIRONMENT

Among the most useful new products are those that enable us to manage pest problems while doing as little damage as possible to beneficial insects and other organisms.

Bacillus thuringiensis **insecticide** products have been around for years now. Common trade names are Dipel, Thuricide and Biotrol. *Bacillus thuringiensis* is a bacterium that only kills certain pests, depending on the specific strain of B.T. used. B.T.-containing products should be our first choice when we're trying to control caterpillar pests. Such B.T. products are only harmful to the caterpillars. There are other B.T. formulations based on a different strain of the bacterium, however, for controlling pests such as mosquito larvae.

Soaps have been used for years to control sucking insects such as aphids, scales and whiteflies. That's why your grandmother may have poured the dishwater over the gardenia bush. Commercially available soap sprays, such as those by Safer, are supposedly more effective than household soaps and less likely to burn the plants.

Insecticides based on azadirachtin, the extract from the **neem** tree, are among the latest of the biorational pesticides. Examples are BioNeem, Margosan-O and Azatin. Pests controlled include whiteflies, thrips, mealybugs, leaf miners, caterpillars, loopers, chinch bugs, sod webworms and aphids. The advantages of the neem-based insecticides are that they have low toxicity to animals and people; do not affect beneficial insects, bees, wasps or earthworms; and have no pest-resistance. However, they are not labeled for edible crops. And, they may be hazardous to fish and other aquatic life.

The neem products act as a growth regulator. They must be sprayed early in the insect's life cycle. They should be applied in early morning or late afternoon when the humidity is high to improve wetting. They should be applied 2-3 times at 7-day intervals.

Horticultural oils are also effective, safe insecticides, effective on aphids, some caterpillars, lacebugs, leafhoppers, mealybugs, mites, scales and whiteflies. However, you need to follow label directions carefully to avoid plant damage. Examples are Volck, Sunspray, Saf-T-Side and Superior Oil.

Even vegetable oil from your kitchen can be used to control insects. Mix 2½ tablespoons with 2½ tablespoons of a mild liquid dishwashing detergent in a gallon of water. However, before using on a number of plants, spray a small area and wait 2-3 days to observe. Some types of plants may be burned by the mixture and you'll want to know before you spray all your plants.

In the not-too-distant past, organic gardeners who didn't want to use traditional "chemical" fertilizers had a difficult time finding a lawn fertilizer that could be spread with a fertilizer spreader. They had to mix materials such as dehydrated cow manure, granite or woodashes and colloidal phosphate or bonemeal. However, now there are **organic fertilizers** already blended into a neat, granular form that can be spread just like any other fertilizer. The primary advantage to using such a fertilizer is that the nutrients release very slowly and over a longer period of time. The primary disadvantage is the cost. A typical analysis is 4-5-4. So it will require higher rates of application than your standard 16-4-8 fertilizer.

Earlier in this book, I encouraged you to leave the clippings on your lawn when you mow. Another new product, the **mulching mower**, makes it easier than ever to let the clippings remain on the lawn. The blades of mulching mowers are designed to whisk the clippings up toward the mower deck above the blade after they are clipped. The clippings then must fall down past the blade again and are cut into smaller pieces.

If you don't want to buy a new mower just to get the mulching feature, check with your dealer. You can put a special mulching blade on many mowers. But if the mower deck isn't also designed properly, with enough space above the blade to float the clippings to be re-cut, the concept doesn't work as well.

Many mulching mowers also give you the option of using a bagger or a side-discharge chute. It's good to have those options at certain times of the year or for certain conditions.

And, finally, whenever you buy a new mower, check to be sure it can be adjusted to mow your lawn as high as you'll need to mow it. Remember, St. Augustine grass needs to be mowed no lower than three inches.

17

For More Information

Other Reading Material that Applies to Our Region

EXTENSION PUBLICATIONS

Many helpful gardening publications are available, free-of-charge from your local county agricultural extension office. When you call, tell them the subject you're interested in, and they'll tell you if they have an appropriate publication. In addition, several for-sale publications are available from the state extension publications center at the University of Florida:

Florida Guide to Environmental Landscapes, $3.00
Pests In and Around the Florida Home, $7.42
Florida Lawn Handbook, $6.00

Contact your county extension office for an order form, or, if you're using Mastercard or Visa, you may phone 1-800-226-1764 Monday through Friday (8 a.m.-noon and 1-5 p.m.)

BOOKS

Garden Guide to the Lower South, published by the Trustees' Garden Club of Savannah, Ga., $12.95. Another good overall garden guide for our area.

Perennial Garden Color, William C. Welch. $29.95. Welch is an extension specialist from Texas, so most of the information applies well to our area.

Antique Roses for the Deep South, William C. Welch. $29.95. If you're interested in old garden roses, this is a good book.

Herbaceous Perennial Plants, Allan M. Armitage. $32.95. A fairly comprehensive listing of perennials, including cultivars. But not all the perennials listed will grow in our area.

Your Florida Garden, Watkins and Wolfe. $13.95. More helpful for the central and southern part of the state, but much of it applies here as well.

Florida Landscape Plants, John V. Watkins and Thomas J. Sheehan. $14.95. Because it covers the whole state, some of the plants will not tolerate our winters.

Know It and Grow It, Carl Whitcomb. $35.00. A guide to the identification and use of woody landscape plants for the South.

Southern Herb Growing, Madalene Hill and Gwen Barclay with Jean Hardy. $29.95.

Butterfly Gardening for the South, Geyata Ajilvsgi, $34.95.

Garden Pools, Fountains and Waterfalls, Southern Living Books. $8.99.

Trees of Northern Florida, Herman Kurz and Robert K. Godfrey. $19.95. Covers native trees only.

124

Trees, Shrubs and Woody Vines of Northern Florida and Adjacent Georgia and Alabama, Robert K. Godfrey. $50.00. Covers natives only.

Gardening with Native Wild Flowers, Samuel B. Jones, Jr., and Leonard E. Foote. $32.95.

Gardening Success with Difficult Soils, Scott Ogden, $18.95. Scott is from Texas, so most of his plant comments apply here, too.

Passalong Plants, Steve Bender and Felder Rushing. $16.95. A closer look at some of the plants typically passed along from generation to generation by gardeners in the South.

The World of Magnolias, Dorothy Callaway. $45.00.

Index

(Botanical names are listed in italics and common names are listed in Roman type. Numbers preceded by "P" indicate color photographs.)

W

Y

Z

NOTES:

Use this convenient form to order additional copies of:

Tallahassee Gardening
DESIGN & CARE OF THE SOUTHERN LANDSCAPE

Please send me _____book(s)

Prices below reflect shipping & handling.

(*Fla. residents add .91¢ Florida sales tax.)

$15.95 Outside Florida x # of books = _____

$16.86 Florida Residents x # of books = _____

NAME _____

ADDRESS_____

CITY _____ STATE _____ ZIP _____

DAYTIME PHONE ( ) _____

Please charge purchase price to my credit card:

Acct. # _____

Signature _____

Expiration Date _____

☐ VISA ☐ DISCOVER

☐ MasterCard

To order by mail, send check, money order or credit card information to:

Tallahassee Gardening
Tallahassee Democrat
P.O. Box 990
Tallahassee, FL 32302

TALLAHASSEE DEMOCRAT